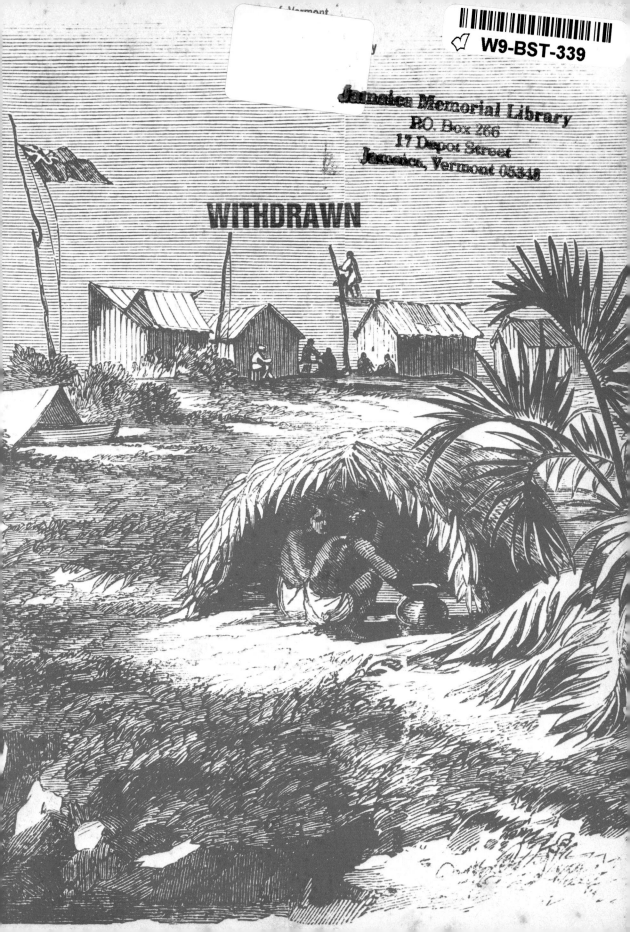

LIVINGSTONE

OVERLEAF LEFT
Portrait of Livingstone
painted at Cambridge
by Monson in December 1851
for Rev. W. Monk.
RIGHT
'Unlocking of Central Africa' –
Dr Livingstone turns the key.
ENDPAPERS
Dr Livingstone's station
at the mouth of
the Kongone river.

LIVINGSTONE

And his African Journeys

Elspeth Huxley

Saturday Review Press
New York

Designed by Juanita Grout *for*
George Weidenfeld and
Nicolson Limited,
11 St John's Hill,
London sw11 *and*
Saturday Review Press,
201 Park Avenue South,
New York, N.Y.10003

Filmset by
Cox & Wyman Ltd,
London, Fakenham
and Reading

ISBN 0–8415–0289–7
Library of Congress
Catalog Card No: 73–87557

Printed in Great Britain

To Charles, Frederica and Jos

Contents

Acknowledgements 6

Introduction 7

1 Called to Africa 10

2 'A Path to the Interior' 36

3 Lone Explorer 60

4 Privation to Prosperity 82

5 Back to the Zambesi 106

6 The Fight against Slavery 138

7 Zanzibar to Ujiji 162

8 To the Ancient Fountains 190

Select Bibliography 218

List of Illustrations 219

Index 222

Acknowledgements

The author and publisher wish to thank Professor George
Shepperson, Mrs D.M.Castle of the Royal Geographical Society,
William Cunningham, Warden of the David Livingstone Trust,
and Mrs Pridmore of the United Society for the Propagation of
the Gospel for their help and co-operation in the preparation of
this book. We would also like to thank Chatto and Windus Ltd. for
access to the copyright works edited by I.Schapera.

Pictures were researched by Philippa Lewis and maps were drawn
by Design Practitioners Limited. We are grateful to the many
official bodies, institutions and individuals for their assistance in
supplying original illustration material.

Introduction

THE STORY OF LIVINGSTONE'S LIFE reveals a man completely dedicated to the things in which he believed; first Christianity, which was the initial driving force, then exploration and natural history, for which missionary zeal provided opportunity to a man so determinedly hard working that little went unrecorded. Above all, he was a good man who laid no blame on others, making up for their shortcomings with his own resolution and an unwavering belief that God would aid in achieving whatever he set out to do. This was not an unreasonable attitude, since no unworthy motives ever entered his head.

He was at his best when travelling alone with Africans, for he showed some inability to organise and control expeditions when he was accompanied by people of his own kind. Throughout more than forty years he sought to teach the Gospel, point out the evils of the slave trade, and extend the world's knowledge of African geography by major discoveries. Only in the last of these was he truly successful during his lifetime, but the emotions aroused by his death were directly responsible for a widespread Christian movement on the continent, and the virtual cessation of the slave trade.

During the period 1840-52 his first preoccupation was to establish missionary settlements in Bechuanaland. In 1844 he married Mary Moffat and five years later, on his second attempt, he crossed the Kalahari Desert to reach Lake Ngami which had never been seen by white men. On a second journey to the same region he took his wife and children, placing their safety, as he did his own, in the hands of God. When his baby daughter died he commented, '. . . we now have one of our number in Heaven'.

Introduction

In 1852 his family returned to England and for the next twelve years he continued his travels alone. In his search for a healthy site for a mission station he reached Luanda and later, following the River Zambesi, discovered the Victoria Falls. From that time, although he constantly thought of himself as a missionary, his activities became increasingly geographical and his thoughts turned constantly to the problem of the source of the Nile.

After a year in England during 1857-8, he returned to Africa to explore the River Shiré and Lake Nyasa. Inevitably he encountered numerous Arab slave traders, but recognised that alone he could do little to stop this evil. Indeed, frequently he was so ill and so destitute that he had to accept their help in order to survive and, surprisingly, they befriended him.

By 1867 he had reached Lake Mweru, and visited Lake Mofwa and the River Lualaba, which he believed to be the upper reaches of the Nile. A year later he discovered Lake Banguelu and then travelled up the west side of Lake Tanganyika before crossing it to Ujiji in March 1869. The following year, despite a long illness, he reached Nyangwe on the Lualaba and witnessed the massacre of many people by slave traders. His reports of this episode reached England and led to determined efforts by the Sultan of Zanzibar to suppress the trade.

By October 1871 he was back in Ujiji where he was found by H.M.Stanley. These two men, very different in character, made a remarkable impression on each other, and together they explored the northern end of Lake Tanganyika before Stanley sadly departed in March 1872.

Livingstone's last journey was a return to Banguelu where

he hoped to by-pass the lake to the south; but his health became worse and worse until on 1 May 1873 he was found dead kneeling by his bed.

To those who know Africa today, or even the Africa of forty years ago, it is difficult to visualise the conditions he encountered, and the incredible fortitude and determination with which he forced his constantly failing body to continue travelling. Somehow acceptable to Africans, enraged by the predatory slavers, without modern medical knowledge, indeed often deprived of any medicines at all, still he persisted. His geographical discoveries and natural history observations provided a great advance in knowledge; but, usually less recognised, is the impact of his reports on the social conscience in Europe. This led to the end of the slave trade, and to the arrival in Africa of a multitude of both missionaries and explorers.

V. E. Fuchs

1 Called to Africa

WHEN, IN 1813 – the year after Napoleon's retreat from Moscow – David Livingstone was born in poverty in a Lanarkshire mill-town, Africa was still the unknown continent. The civilisation of ancient Egypt had scarcely extended its influence south of the Nile's second cataract, on the present boundary with Sudan. The wide barrier of the Sahara lay between the Mediterranean world of North Africa with its Moslem-Arab culture, and the jungles, swamps and tangled waterways with their Negro and Pygmy peoples of the unexplored tropical centre. In the south, Europeans had occupied the Cape since 1652, but by the beginning of the nineteenth century had advanced no further north than the Orange river. Beyond it lay the Kalahari Desert which was thought to form one with the Sahara. On the eastern side, European penetration had been halted by the warlike and well-organised Zulu people – Caffres as they were called – and their satellites.

Something was known of the coastal regions on either side. The ancient Arab sea-ports dotted along the east coast from Mogadiscio to Sofala had been taken over, with a good deal of changing hands, by the Portuguese. (Zanzibar remained Arab.) The Portuguese had made little serious attempt to probe the interior; the furthest inland post they maintained was at Tete, about three hundred miles up the Zambesi river. On the west, European slaving stations had been established from the sixteenth century onwards, but the traders had no need to penetrate inland; the slaves came to them. Out of the anti-slavery movement of the eighteenth century arose, in 1788, the African Association, formed for the express purpose of exploring the interior. Its founders acted on the belief that Livingstone would come to share: that exploration would lead to civilisation, which would put an end to the slave-trade and open a way for Christianity. In 1795 Mungo Park reached the Niger overland from near the mouth of the Gambia river, returning in 1805 to navigate about a thousand miles of its upper reaches before perishing in its waters.

Many geographers shared Park's view that the Niger and the Congo were one, and it was not until David Livingstone was seven years old that Richard Lander traced the Niger's passage to the sea and so disproved this theory. Thus the Niger became the first and, until Livingstone's journey down the Zambesi, the only one of Africa's great rivers whose course had been charted by European explorers. The one partial exception

PREVIOUS PAGES On these wide and sun-drenched Bechuana plains Robert Moffat and his wife Mary created an extensive mission and set an example of Christian living.

was the discovery in 1770 by James Bruce of the source, in Ethiopia, of the Blue Nile.

This, very briefly, was the state of European knowledge of Africa's interior when David Livingstone was a boy. He was an avid reader, and the great sagas of Bruce and Mungo Park, Denham, Clapperton and the Lander brothers, best-sellers of their day, would have come his way. From them he would have learned how much remained to be discovered; how great was the need to spread civilisation into dark places; and how dangerous was the challenge. Sickness, starvation, pain and very often death was the lot of the explorer. Forty-five Europeans started off on Park's second expedition to the Niger; not a single one returned.

But it was not for exploration that David Livingstone wished to leave his native Scotland, nor to Africa that he wished to go. He wanted to become a missionary and to go to China. He was born in Blantyre, Lanarkshire, on 19 March 1813, the second son of Neil Livingston (the 'e' was added later) and Agnes Hunter. The Livingstons were originally crofters from the island of Ulva, by Mull. David's great-grandfather fell at Culloden, and his grandfather, also Neil, emigrated with his family in 1792 to Clydebank where the industrial revolution was drawing impoverished crofters into 'dark satanic mills' and soul-destroying wage-slavery. But how soul-destroying? Certainly the souls of the Livingstones were not destroyed. Four of Neil's sons served in the Napoleonic wars; the fifth, David's father, Neil the younger, became a clerk and then an itinerant tea-vendor. 'Too conscientious ever to become rich', as his son wrote of him, he was also an intensely religious man, and distributed tracts along with packets of tea.

The family home was a single room, fourteen feet by ten, in a three-storey tenement. There were two beds, each in a recess, one for the parents, the other for the children. Here Neil and Agnes Livingston procreated, raised, fed, cleaned and cared for seven children, two of whom died in infancy. Space must have been found for books, for all were great readers. Neil favoured religious works. He held office as deacon in an independent Congregational church at Hamilton, three miles away. The whole family would walk to it on Sundays, taking their provisions and refusing to accept from fellow-worshippers any more hospitality than 'a kettle of boiling water for tea and seats at the table for the family'. After David married, he wrote

LEFT Mary and Robert Moffat, whose daughter
Livingstone was later to marry. The Moffats
translated the whole of the Bible and
The Pilgrim's Progress into Sechwana, but
when Livingstone arrived they had not made
a convert in five years.

ABOVE Livingstone's first
posting as a missionary
was to Kuruman in
Bechuanaland, founded by
the London Missionary
Society in 1818.

to his mother: 'Only yesterday I said to my wife, when I thought of the nice clean bed I now enjoy, "You put me in mind of my mother; she was always particular about our beds and linen."' The words 'poor and pious' which he caused to be inscribed on their tombstone epitomised their lives.

At the age of ten, David went to work as a cotton piecer. With his first week's wages he bought a Latin grammar, propped it up on the frame of a spinning-jenny and memorised sentences as he walked to and fro tying broken ends of thread. His hours were 6 a.m. to 8 p.m. with two breaks for meals. 'I

kept up a pretty constant study undisturbed by the roar of the machinery.' To this he owed his power of 'completely abstracting the mind from surrounding noises, so as to read and write with perfect comfort amid the play of children or the dances and songs of savages'.

From 8 p.m. until 10 p.m. he continued his Latin studies under a schoolmaster, and after ten, at home, 'the dictionary part of my labours was followed up till twelve o'clock, or later, if my mother did not interfere by jumping up and snatching the books out of my hands'. Then back to work by six next morning. On his rare holidays he would roam the surrounding countryside, armed with *Culpepper's Herbal*, to collect specimens of plants, insects and fossils, thus laying the foundations of a knowledge of natural history that was to remain his lifelong pleasure. Sometimes he went fishing, and at least once poached a salmon. Now and again he worked for a farmer, who later commented: 'I didn'a think muckle o' that David Livingston – he was aye lyin' on his belly readin' a book.' He read everything he could lay his hands on except novels – works on science and travel being his first choice.

At about the age of twenty he experienced what cannot be called a conversion, since religious beliefs implanted in infancy had never wavered; rather it was the dawn of a conviction that he himself, as an individual Christian, should

ABOVE At the age of ten David went to work a twelve-hour day in a cotton-spinning factory, and while acting as a piecer taught himself Latin and Greek amid the clatter of machinery.

OPPOSITE Released from the factory at 8 p.m., he continued his studies under a school-master, Mr Skimming, until 10 p.m., when 'the dictionary part' of his labours in his home occupied his time until midnight.

While continuing to work in the cotton mills in summer to earn his tuition, in the winter months David studied medicine, Greek and divinity at Anderson's College, Glasgow, to fit himself to become a medical missionary in China.

actively and personally enter into the service of God. 'The perfect freeness with which the pardon of all our guilt is offered in God's book', he wrote, 'drew forth feelings of affectionate love to Him who bought us with His blood, and a sense of deep obligation to Him for His mercy has influenced, in some small measure, my conduct ever since. . . . In the glow of love which Christianity inspires, I soon resolved to devote my life to the alleviation of human misery.' Therefore he would qualify as a doctor, and go as a medical missionary to China.

While continuing to work as a cotton-spinner in summer, for two winters he attended lectures in medicine, Greek and Divinity at Anderson's College in Glasgow, for a fee of £12 a year. The assistant to the professor of chemistry, James Young, became his closest friend. Young was later to invent the process which gave rise to paraffin, and to befriend his old student in so many ways that Livingstone named a river after him and expressed the wish to 'lie beside him' if he died at home. To

Young, Livingstone was 'the best man I ever knew'. In 1837, he applied to the London Missionary Society for employment and was accepted on probation a year later. His apprenticeship was served at Chipping Ongar in Essex. One of his fellow-students remembered him thus:

Livingstone stood middle-sized, firm upon his feet, light in the under-trunk, round and full in the chest. I have to admit he was 'no bonny'. His face wore at all times the strongly marked lines of potent will. I never recollect of him relaxing into the abandon of youthful frolic or play. I would by no means imply sourness of temper. It was the strength of a resolute man of work.

How resolute, can be judged by an episode related by another fellow student, Joseph Moore. David's elder brother John was working for a Hamilton lace-dealer. In order to help him, David set out at three o'clock one foggy November morning to walk twenty-seven miles to London, and fell into a ditch on the way. Chilled, soaked and dirty, he spent the whole day calling at lace-dealing shops and merchants in the City. In the evening he walked back, encountering *en route* an unconscious lady who had been thrown from a gig. He helped to carry her to a house, examined her, summoned a doctor and continued on his way, which he missed, and wandered among the woods and marshes to reach his lodgings after midnight, exhausted but with his mission accomplished.

While his sincerity and devotion were never in question, Livingstone was a clumsy preacher with a rough, sometimes indistinct voice, and received at the end of his probation an adverse report. Only a single vote on the Society's Board of Directors won him a further period of probation. The Principal's final report, while not enthusiastic, sufficed to get this rough diamond of a Glaswegian the benefit of the doubt:

Mr Livingstone gives me pleasure in some important respects. The objection I mentioned, his heaviness of manner, united as it is with a rusticity, not likely to be removed, still strikes me as having importance, but he has sense and quiet vigour; his temper is good and his character substantial, so that I do not like the thought of his being rejected. Add to his stock of knowledge and then I trust he will prove after all an instrument worth having – a diligent, staunch, single-hearted labourer. If the decision were now coming on I should say accept him.

One further quote can be cited, again from his friend Joseph

Moore, to indicate how Livingstone appeared to his contemporaries at this time when, aged twenty-six, he stood on the threshold of his career:

I grew daily more attached to him. If I were asked why, I should be rather at a loss to reply. There was a truly indescribable charm about him which, with all his rather ungainly ways and by no means winning face, attracted almost everyone. . . . He won those who came near him by a kind of spell. There happened to be in the boarding house at that time a young M.D., a saddler from Hants, and a bookseller from Scotland. To this hour they all speak of him in rapturous terms.

This uncouth charm worked its magic across all boundaries of race and nation. Absolute honesty, sincerity, modesty and courage – these were among the ingredients. There was also compassion: 'He was so kind and gentle in word and deed to all about him that all loved him.' He could also be obstinate, opinionated and demanding. It is no use trying to pin down the formula. It worked with his fellow-students in Essex when he was young and it worked on his African companions in the desolate swamps of central Africa when he was a stricken, spent old man.

After finishing at Ongar, he took lodgings in Aldersgate Street in London and continued his medical studies in order to qualify as a doctor, working partly at the Charing Cross and Moorfields hospitals. His ideas were still centred on China, but an opium war there was holding matters up. The turning-point of Livingstone's career came when he made the acquaintance of Robert Moffat, one of the great missionaries of Africa, who stayed for a short time at the Aldersgate boarding house.

I observed soon that this young man was interested in my story, that he would sometimes come quietly and ask me a question or two. . . . By and by he asked me whether I thought he would do for Africa. I said I believed he would, if he would not go to an old station, but would advance to unoccupied ground, specifying the vast plain to the north, where I had sometimes seen, in the morning sun, the smoke of a thousand villages, where no missionary had ever been. At last Livingstone said: 'What is the use of my waiting for the end of this abominable opium war? I will go at once to Africa.' The Directors concurred, and Africa became his sphere.

In November 1840, Livingstone qualified as a Licentiate of

the Royal Faculty of Physicians and Surgeons in Glasgow, but could spend only one night at Blantyre before starting on the journey from which he might never return. 'On the morning of 17th November,' his sister wrote, 'we got up at five o'clock. My mother made coffee. David read the 121st and 135th Psalms, and prayed. My father and he walked to Glasgow to catch the Liverpool steamer.' Father and son never met again. Three days later, David was ordained in Albion Chapel, London Wall, a ceremony to which, curiously enough, he was indifferent: 'I do not attach any importance to ordination.' On 8 December 1840, he embarked in the sailing ship *George* for the Cape. On the voyage, the Captain taught him how to use the quadrant and to fix positions by the stars, a skill which was to prove indispensable in his travels. From Port Elizabeth a journey by ox-wagon of more than seven hundred miles – 'so pleasant that I never got tired of it' – brought him and a fellow novice across

Port Elizabeth in South Africa, painted by the artist Thomas Baines seven years after Livingstone landed there to take up his post in Bechuanaland, distant by a further three months' journey in an ox-wagon.

the Orange river, and so to Kuruman in Bechuanaland (now Botswana).

Kuruman, controlled since 1823 by Robert Moffat, was the *ultima Thule* of missionary endeavour in South Africa. Beyond lay 'the smoke of a thousand villages'; souls awaiting redemption; the Kalahari Desert that no white man had crossed; and beyond that, all of unknown Africa. David Livingstone was then twenty-eight years old; a qualified doctor as well as a clergyman; his salary, £75 a year; his deepest ambition 'to preach beyond another man's lines'. Moffat's advice had sunk in, no doubt because it accorded so completely with his own desires. He wanted to be the first missionary to carry the word of God into new lands.

Robert Moffat had been a gardener by trade before he became a missionary, and at Kuruman he and his wife created a garden out of a wilderness. With its fenced and irrigated vegetable beds, its flowering trees and shrubs, its neatly-built thatched houses and its carpentry shed, smithy and stockaded cattle-pen, Kuruman was a pleasant spot – too pleasant, or at least too civilised; not what the young evangelist had come to Africa to find. Within two months he was off in an ox-wagon

24

with a colleague and two native converts on a trek of seven hundred miles to the north-east, 'further in that direction than any missionaries have yet been'. Here he began to learn some of the hard truths of his calling. He wrote to an Ongar friend: 'Don't expect to find chiefs friendly to missionaries. In general they are hostile, and when friendly it is generally for the purpose of "milking" them.' He added: 'Don't forget a good gun and how to use it. Also some carpentry – with tools.'

After a short interlude at Kuruman, he set out again alone with two ox-drivers and two converts and camped among the Bakwena, one of the numerous Bechuana tribes. 'Here, in order to obtain an accurate knowledge of the language, I cut myself off from all European society for about six months, and gained by this ordeal an insight into the habits, ways of thinking, laws, and language, which has proved of incalculable advantage in my intercourse with them ever since.' He gained also a knowledge of their diseases: 'sometimes my wagon was quite besieged by the blind and halt and lame', and people came for two hundred miles and more for treatment.

A second object of this journey, which covered about one

Before the days of railways, covered Cape wagons, drawn by spans of up to sixteen oxen, were the only means of transport. In a wagon such as this, Livingstone travelled 700 miles to reach Kuruman averaging about eight miles a day.

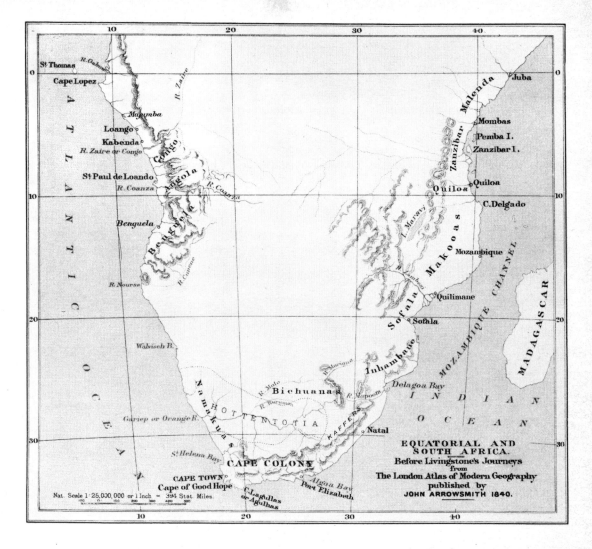

EQUATORIAL AND
SOUTH AFRICA.
Before Livingstone's Journeys
from
The London Atlas of Modern Geography
published by
JOHN ARROWSMITH 1840.

Nat. Scale 1:25,000,000 or 1 inch = 394 Stat. Miles.

thousand miles, was to select a site for a new mission station. He had been dismayed at the sparseness of the population round Kuruman, at the few converts – Moffat had not made one for five years – and at the contentment of his colleagues to stay there in considerable comfort, saying 'perhaps the time for the people of the interior has not yet come'. South Africa, he concluded, was 'overstocked with missionaries', while to the north lay the vast unknown where no missionary had ever been.

Early in 1843, he camped at the village of the paramount chief of the Bakwena, whose only son was sick with dysentery, which Livingstone was able to cure. Thus began a fruitful

Africa south of the equator before Livingstone arrived in 1841. Until his journeys, little more was known than had been known or surmised for hundreds of years.

friendship between the missionary and this remarkable chief, Sechele. 'I was from the first struck by his intelligence, and by the marked manner in which we both felt drawn to each other.' Sechele listened to the message of redemption with an attention all too rare among his people, but then inquired – 'Do you imagine these people will ever believe by your merely talking to them? I can make them do nothing except by thrashing them; if you like, I shall call my head men, and with our *litupa* [rhinoceros-hide whips], we will soon make them all believe together.' Like Moffat before him, Sechele fired the imagination of the young missionary. Pointing north towards the Kalahari Desert, he said: 'You never can cross that country to the tribes beyond; it is utterly impossible even for us black men, except in certain seasons, when more than the usual supply of rain falls, and an extraordinary growth of water-melons follows.'

When his ox-drivers refused to go further north for fear of Matabele raiders, Livingstone was 'reduced to the necessity of either giving up my tour and returning, or going forward on ox-back. I chose the latter. . . .' It was not a comfortable mode of travel. An ox could not be saddled, and with a sweep of his wide horns could, and often did, catch his rider a smart blow in the side or stomach. Livingstone rode about four hundred miles sitting as bolt upright as a dragoon to avoid the horns. He went hungry and thirsty, living on locusts and honey, and on moisture sucked through reeds from under the sand. By evening camp-fires he listened to tribal tales and 'intermingled the story of the Cross with their conversation'. This was his true initiation into the realities of African travel.

Having selected a mission site at Mabotsa, about 220 miles north of Kuruman – 'a lovelier spot you never saw' – in 1843 he made his camp there with a colleague, Roger Edwards, and started to build a large hut and dig a watercourse. Before it was completed he joined a party of Bechuana on a hunt for lions that had been preying on their cattle. The sequel is best told in his own words:

In going round the end of the hill I saw one of the beasts sitting on a piece of rock as before, but this time he had a little bush in front. Being about thirty yards off, I took a good aim at his body through the bush, and fired both barrels into it. . . . I saw the lion's tail erected in anger behind the bush, and, turning to the people, said, 'Stop a little till I load again.' When in the act of ramming down the bullets I heard a shout. Starting, and looking half round, I saw the lion just in the act of springing upon me. I was upon a little height; he caught my shoulder as he sprang, and we both came to the ground below together. Growling horribly close to my ear, he shook me as a terrier dog does a rat. The shock produced a stupor similar to that which seems to be felt by a mouse after the first shake of the cat. It caused a sort of dreaminess, in which there was no sense of pain nor feeling of terror, though quite conscious of all that was happening. It was like what patients partially under the influence of chloroform describe, who see all the operation, but feel not the knife. This singular condition was not the result of any mental process. The shake annihilated fear, and allowed no sense of horror in looking round at the beast. This peculiar state is probably produced in all animals killed by the carnivora; and if so, is a merciful provision by our benevolent Creator for lessening the pain of death.

Turning round to relieve myself of the weight, as he had one paw on the back of my head, I saw his eyes directed to Mebalwe, who was trying to shoot him at a distance of ten or fifteen yards. His gun, a flint one, missed fire in both barrels; the lion immediately left me, and attacking Mebalwe, bit his thigh. Another man, whose life I had saved before after he had been tossed by a buffalo, attempted to spear the lion while he was biting Mebalwe. He left Mebalwe and caught this man by the shoulder, but at that moment the bullets he had received took effect, and he fell down dead. . . . I had on a tartan jacket on this occasion, and I believe that it wiped off all the virus from the teeth that pierced the flesh, for my two companions in this affray have both suffered from the peculiar pains, while I have escaped with only the inconvenience of a false joint in my limb.

It was typical of Livingstone to dismiss the affair as of small account, but to a friend he wrote: 'Besides crunching the bone into splinters, he left eleven teeth wounds on the upper part of my arm.' Without, of course, an anaesthetic, Edwards did his best to dress the wound and set the splintered bone. 'His sufferings were dreadful', Edwards wrote. Livingstone himself admitted that the wound was 'both painful and protracted', as the bone fragments did not quickly unite and 'every motion of the body produced a grating irritation which reacted on the wounds'. For the rest of his life, he was never able to raise his left arm above the shoulder, nor support one of the heavy double-barrelled muzzle-loaders of the day with his damaged arm.

When he was well enough to travel, he returned to Kuruman where the Moffats took him under their care. It fell mainly to

'Starting, and looking half around, I saw the lion just in the act of springing upon me.'

"GROWLING HORRIBLY, HE SHOOK ME AS A TERR

OG DOES A RAT."

At Mabotsa, 220 miles north of Kuruman, Livingstone joined a hunting party and a wounded lion mauled him so severely that he was never able afterwards to raise his left arm above the shoulder.

31

their eldest daughter Mary to nurse him, and the outcome was predictable. On a day in July 1844, 'I screwed up my courage to put a question beneath one of the fruit-trees, the result of which was that I became united in marriage to Mr Moffat's eldest daughter Mary. Having been born in the country and being an expert in household matters, she was always the best spoke in the wheel at home.' She was twenty-three years old: 'not romantic, but a matter-of-fact lady, a little, black-haired girl, sturdy, and all that I want'. Despite this prosaic approach, there is no doubt that they were deeply in love. Only in one letter was this admitted: 'It will comfort all your hearts to know that I am become as great a fool as any of you. . . . In love! words, yea, thoughts fail. . . .'

Marriage, in January 1845, brought an automatic rise in salary – to £100 a year. With this Livingstone built their first home at Mabotsa; a mud-walled shed fifty-two feet by twenty, roofed with reeds. Their sojourn here was brief. A quarrel flared up with Edwards, a considerably older man, and Livingstone left the new station to his colleague – 'a fiery old gent'. They moved about forty miles further north to Sechele's headquarters at Chonuane, and built another rough dwelling. Here their first child, Robert Moffat, was born in 1846. He was only a few months old when the family set out by ox-wagon in an easterly direction, to survey the mission field. When they crossed the headwaters of the Limpopo river, for the first time they encountered fear and hostility among the people. The Bagalaka (another Bechuana tribe) mistook them for Boers, who were taking possession of land and 'fountains' (springs) and claiming the whole country as their own. From the start, Livingstone was up in arms against the Boers who, in his opinion, were enslaving Africans by a combination of forced unpaid labour, and of downright pillage. They did not regard Africans as fellow human beings: 'One told me tonight "as well teach baboons". I proposed a trial of reading and writing between one of these baboons and himself, and he soon drew in his horns.'

Back at Kuruman their second child, Agnes, was born in 1847. Not long afterwards, the family made yet another move, this time from Chonuane, which was subject to terrible droughts, to a healthier site on the Kolobeng river about forty miles further north. Sechele moved his whole village there. Kolobeng did prove reasonably healthy but hardly peaceful;

rhinos 'not infrequently come by mistake rushing through the town'. It was a hard, self-sufficient life. 'My rib bakes all our bread' – in an ant-hill; she also made their candles, soap and clothing, looked after her babies and taught in an infants' school. No wonder that by the end of a day which started at six and ended with a prayer-meeting at 8.30 or 9 p.m., everyone was too tired for mental exertion. 'I am becoming more and more of a barbarian', Livingstone wrote.

A missionary in Africa, he had by this time discovered, had to spend a great deal more of his time as a rough carpenter, joiner, blacksmith, mason and jack-of-all-trades than as a saver of souls. His correspondence with his father-in-law at Kuruman, 270 miles away – conveyed erratically by ox-wagon or sometimes by itinerant Hottentots who charged a calf for carrying a letter – is full of such pleas as: 'Could you spare me a bottle of linseed oil?', 'Please send a bit of old copper for soldering', and requests for scrap iron, bullet moulds, door-bolts and cold chisels. He grudged the time spent on these routine and sometimes physically painful tasks, and was saddened by the fact, which he faced with characteristic honesty, that his message fell on almost wholly deaf ears.

In his apprentice days, he had taken it for granted that the good news he would carry to the heathen would be welcomed like a rising sun dispelling the darkness of a long night. Nothing of the sort occurred. Darkness was what the heathens seemed to prefer. Moffat, after nearly thirty years among the Bechuana, wrote that 'they treated with ridicule and contempt the truths which are delivered'. His son-in-law found this only too true: 'They have not the smallest love for the gospel of Jesus, they hate and fear it as a revolutionary spirit is disliked by the old Tories.' He 'never went to a meeting without a sense of oppression on my spirits', finding among his small and bored congregation 'less indication of interest than if all had been idle tales'.

There was, however, one bright spot and that was Sechele, who had been genuinely moved by the Christian message. Wisely, his white mentor did not try to hurry his conversion. It was seven years, and after a distressing lapse involving one of his many wives whom the chief was obliged to return to their parents, before Sechele was baptised. He was almost the only whole-hearted convert Livingstone ever made.

In April 1849, at Kolobeng, a third child was born and

A journey to the north-east in 1846 brought Livingstone into contact with the Boers, tough and aggressive Afrikaner farmers who, with their families and wagons, were spreading northwards from the British-governed Cape to establish republics in what were to become the Transvaal and Orange Free State.

named Thomas Steele after one of a trio of young sportsmen on leave from India who had travelled in company with Livingstone in 1843. On their journey from the Cape to Kuruman, these sportsmen had spent £1,000 and 'all they will take away will be a few skins and heads of animals'. Livingstone despised big game shooting, and never killed an animal himself except for food or in self-defence. Not only that, these young officers were 'men of the world who would travel on Sundays if we were not with them'. Despite this, he became fast friends with Captain Steele of the Coldstream Guards, the 'politest of them' who was well versed in the classics. It was a friendship that was to endure, as almost all his friendships did, for the rest of his life.

Sechele, chief of the Bakwena tribe, was Livingstone's principal friend and supporter among the Bechuana, and possibly his only sincere convert. On his baptism Sechele had to give back to their fathers all his numerous wives except the first and eldest.

2 'A Path to the Interior'

IN THE FAR NORTH beyond the Kalahari Desert – so Sechele told his white friend – lived the powerful and benevolent ruler Sebituane (in modern spelling Sebetwane), chief of the Makololo tribe. Sechele urged Livingstone to visit him. 'This was the first time', the missionary wrote, 'I had thought of crossing the desert to Lake Ngami.' The existence of this large lake was known to Europeans only by repute; none had seen it.

The Kalahari was called a desert only because it had no springs and few wells; normally it was covered with grass, bush and a great variety of creeping plants. There was game in abundance, and two kinds of human inhabitant: the Bushmen

RIGHT Among the rich young sportsmen who visited Bechuanaland to hunt big game was William Cotton Oswell, then on leave from India. He and Livingstone struck up a friendship which lasted for the rest of the missionary's life.

PREVIOUS PAGES Lake Ngami, subsequently painted by Thomas Baines, was the first of Livingstone's geographical discoveries and earned him recognition from the Royal Geographical Society.

and a degenerate Bechuana tribe, the Bakalahari. Many of the plants had large tuberous roots which stored moisture, and in exceptionally wet seasons a kind of water-melon carpeted whole tracts of country and delighted every species from ele-phants to mice with its succulent juices. The Bakalahari women sucked subterranean water through reeds into ostrich egg-shells, which they buried, and dug up to sustain them through long droughts. It could be so hot that centipedes emerging from their holes were roasted alive.

In 1845 William Cotton Oswell, a young man on leave from India, had spent two days at Mabotsa before embarking on a three-month shooting safari. His brief acquaintance with Livingstone during that time was the prelude to a lifelong friendship between the two men. In almost every way they were poles apart. Oswell was an aristocrat: tall and good-looking, polished and intelligent, a scholar sportsman, gay and generous of heart. But certain qualities they did share: courage and endurance, integrity, kindness, cheerfulness in adversity and the same high moral code. That was no doubt why Living-stone, with all his prickly Scots independence, was willing to accept Oswell's offer to travel at his expense, and why Oswell felt it a privilege to share his wagons with 'the best, most intelligent and most modest of the missionaries'.

So, on 1 June 1849, a party set out from Kolobeng consisting of Oswell; his friend Mungo Murray; a trader, J. H. Wilson; Livingstone; eight Hottentots; and about thirty Bakwena, equipped with several wagons, eighty oxen, twenty horses and supplies for a year. On the first part of the journey, they lost the way and would have died of thirst had they not spotted a Bushman woman whom Oswell headed off on horseback and who led them to a spring. About half-way across, they came to a broad river, the Zouga, and learned that it flowed out of a lake to the north-east. They followed it up in dug-out canoes, while the wagons advanced with difficulty along the forested bank. On paddling past the mouth of a tributary, Livingstone was told that it came 'from a country full of rivers – so many no one can tell their number – full of large trees'. He was so excited by this unexpected information – the first whisper of Barotseland – that when they actually reached Lake Ngami 'the discovery seemed of little importance'.

In a sense, this was true. The lake, first seen on 1 August 1849, was a shallow, reed-fringed sheet of water about seventy

OPPOSITE Accompanied by
Oswell, two other Europeans
and a party of Hottentots,
Livingstone crossed the
Kalahari and sighted Lake
Ngami on 1 August 1849.
But an unfriendly chief
refused to supply food and
guides to continue the
journey and they were forced
to retreat. The following
year he returned (opposite)
with Mary and their three
small children.

miles in circumference and was gradually drying up. In the
course of the next century, it was to shrink to a residual swamp.
But it lay on a route to the unexplored interior that might be
opened up. It was this prospect that Livingstone immediately
seized upon. If the Bakalahari were right, far to the north lay a
fertile land of rivers, forests and people, many people, quite
unvisited by Europeans. Here indeed were souls awaiting
salvation 'beyond another man's lines'. But the immediate
goal, Sebituane's country, was still two hundred miles further
north. A surly lakeside chief refused to supply guides or food,
and the frustrated expedition, unable to proceed without them,
had to make its laborious way back to Kolobeng.

On his second attempt to reach Sebituane, Livingstone
took his family, although Mary was again pregnant and the
children were aged only four, three and just over one year.
For this he was much criticised. Dangers and hardships there
certainly were, but in Livingstone's defence it may be said that
Mary was well accustomed to both. Wagons were the normal
vehicles of African travel; her husband was a doctor with a
well-stocked medicine chest; on his first visit, the Lake Ngami
region had not seemed unhealthy; and Mary herself may well
have refused to be left alone at the isolated mission with failing
water supplies, serious risks of raids by Boers and no one to
turn to if things went wrong.

They left, accompanied by Sechele but not this time by
Oswell, on 26 April 1850, and made for the north bank of the
Zouga, where progress was difficult and slow. 'The children had
little choice of food on the long 1,200 miles journey', which
lasted four months and ten days. 'In some parts we had to travel
both day and night continuously for want of water, and then
tie up the oxen to prevent them running away till we had dug
wells. I lost four in pitfalls made for game, two from drought,
one by a lion.' When they reached the lake, the unfriendly
chief fell in love with Livingstone's favourite gun, and it was
bartered for a promise of guides.

On the morning he was due to start for Sebituane's, the two
elder children went down with fever, and the next day nearly
all his men were sick. The lake region had proved to be infested
with mosquitoes of a particularly venomous kind. 'Sleep is out
of the question when you come to a den of them. I could not
touch a square half-inch on the bodies of the children unbitten
after a single night's exposure.' It was here that he proved the

worth of his remedy for malaria, evolved by trial and error, which reduced to low proportions the mortality, formerly so crushing, among Europeans. It was a mixture of resin of jalap and calomel (each eight grains) with rhubarb and quinine (each four grains), followed by frequent doses of quinine (four grains) until the fever subsided. Everyone got safely back to Kolobeng, and in August, Mary gave birth to their fourth child. Soon afterwards she had a stroke which partially paralysed her face. The paralysis subsided, but for some time her legs were stiff and painful. Worse still, the baby, a girl, contracted inflammation of the lungs. 'We could not apply remedies to one so young, except the simplest. She uttered a piercing cry, and went away to see the King in His beauty....' Any self-reproach her father may have felt found no expression in his journal: 'It was the first death in our family, but just as likely to have happened had we remained at home, and we have now one of our number in heaven.' But a letter to his father-in-law hints at greater sensitivity: 'It was like tearing out one's bowels to see her in the embrace of the King of Terrors.'

Eight months later, although Mary was pregnant yet again,

On their journey to Lake Ngami and back Livingstone, Oswell and a friend Mungo Murray saw and described two species of antelope new to science, the lechwe and the poku, inhabitants of marshes and riverbanks.

the whole family set out on a third attempt to reach the Makololo chief. Livingstone was more than ever anxious to find a healthy site for a mission station north of Kolobeng and out of range of the Boers, who believed that he was secretly arming the Bechuana in order to resist the Voortrekkers' advance into the Transvaal. Boer threats to wipe out Kolobeng were a potent reason for again exposing his family to the risks of a journey into the unknown. Not that he was without misgivings:

It is a venture to take wife and children where fever – African fever – prevails. But who that believes in Jesus would refuse to make a venture for such a Captain? A parent's heart alone can feel as I do when I look at my little ones and ask, shall I return with this or that one alive? However, we are His and wish to have no interests apart from those of His kingdom and glory.

On another occasion he had written: 'I shall not stop till my breath does, whatever be the consequences' – to others, he might have added, as well as to himself. But he summed it all up in a letter to his father: 'I am a missionary, heart and soul. God had an only Son, and He was a missionary and a physician. A poor, poor imitation of Him I am, or wish to be. In this service I hope to live, in it I wish to die.'

So, in April 1851, the whole family set off with Oswell, who again provided oxen and wagons, diverging from their former route along the Zouga to leave Lake Ngami on their left. The wagons creaked across a dead-flat, waterless plain where Bushmen were encountered: 'wonderful people . . . always merry and laughing and never telling lies wantonly like the Bechuana'. They might not tell lies but they were scarcely reliable. One called Shobo who volunteered to guide them across a featureless belt of sun-scorched, prickly scrub, lost his way, led them on false trails in all directions and finally sat down in the bush saying 'No water, all country, Shobo sleeps' and did so; and shortly afterwards, disappeared.

All they could do was to plod on northwards, their oxen exhausted and their water-bottles almost dry. At last birds were sighted, and the spoor of a rhinoceros. The oxen were unyoked and made off into the bush. Darkness fell, their water was down to the last dregs and the children were suffering. 'This was a bitterly anxious night; and the next morning the less there was of water, the more thirsty the little rogues became. The idea

While trekking across the Kalahari Desert the party encountered wandering bands of nomadic Bushmen, the oldest inhabitants of South Africa. These small, yellow-skinned people had been driven by the more advanced, land-hungry tribes from their former hunting-grounds into arid regions where no crops would grow, and had adapted themselves to the desert.

of their perishing before our eyes was terrible.' On the following afternoon, the fifth of their ordeal, Livingstone's belief in God's protection was confirmed. The drivers returned with 'a supply of that fluid of which we had never before felt the true value'. The oxen had found a stream. Soon afterwards, the unabashed Shobo turned up, halted the caravan demanding tobacco and a light and 'coolly sat down and smoked his pipe'. Instead of being angry, the travellers were amused by his effrontery; 'we all liked Shobo', Livingstone wrote.

They reached at last the vast, swampy regions of the central watershed where Sebituane's territory lay. The chief himself came four hundred miles to greet them and the meeting took place on an island in the Chobe river. Strangely enough 'this really great chief', as Oswell described him, 'a gentleman in thought and manner', who had so much wanted the white men to come, was at first ill at ease. He killed an ox for them, gave them honey and welcomed them, but 'a sad, half-scared look never faded from his face'. Then an odd incident occurred, recounted by Oswell:

44

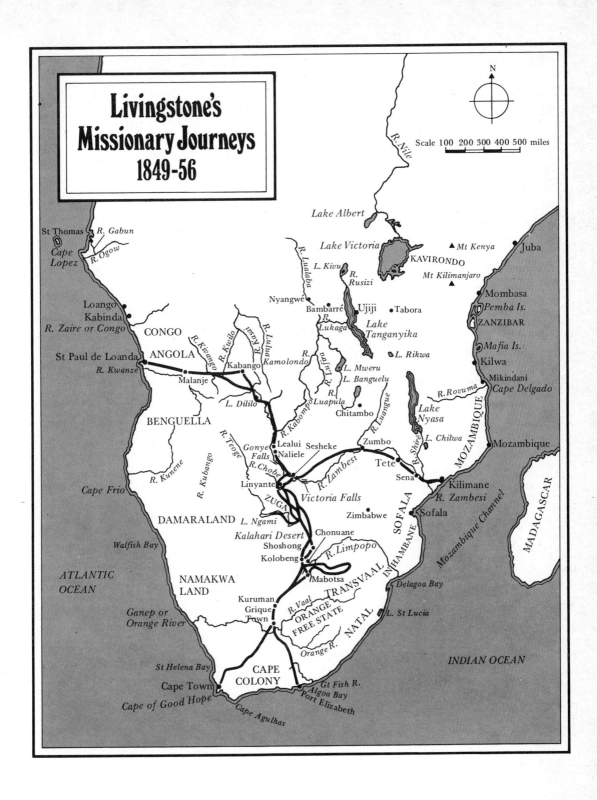

Livingstone's Missionary Journeys 1849-56

N

Scale 100 200 300 400 500 miles

St Thomas *R. Gabun*
Cape Lopez *R. Ogow*
Loango
Kabinda
R. Zaire or Congo CONGO
St Paul de Loanda ANGOLA
R. Kwanze Kabango
Malanje
R. Kwango *R. Kwilo* *R. Kasai*
BENGUELLA *L. Dililo*
R. Kunene *R. Teoge* Gonye Falls Lealui Seseke
Cape Frio *R. Kubango* *R. Chobe* Naliele
Linyante ZUGA *Victoria Falls*
Walfish Bay DAMARALAND *L. Ngami*
Kalahari Desert Chonuane
Shoshong
Kolobeng *R. Limpopo*
NAMAKWA Mabotsa
LAND Kuruman TRANSVAAL
Ganep or Orange River Grique Town *R. Vaal* ORANGE FREE STATE NATAL
Orange R.
St Helena Bay CAPE COLONY
Cape Town
Cape of Good Hope Algoa Bay
Cape Agulhas Port Elizabeth

Lake Albert
Lake Victoria KAVIRONDO ▲ *Mt Kenya* Juba
R. Lualaba *L. Kivu* *R. Rusizi* *Mt Kilimanjaro* ▲
Nyangwé Bambarré Ujiji Tabora Mombasa
R. Lukaga Lake Tanganyika *Pemba Is.* ZANZIBAR
R. Lufira *Mafia Is.*
Kamolondo *L. Mweru* *L. Rikwa* Kilwa
R. Kabompo *L. Banguelu* Mikindani
R. Luapula *R. Rovuma* *Cape Delgado*
Chitambo Lake Nyasa
R. Luangue *L. Chilwa* Mozambique
Zumbo *R. Shire* MOZAMBIQUE
Tete
Sena Kilimane
Zimbabwe SOFALA *R. Zambesi*
R. Zambesi Sofala
INHAMBANE *Mozambique Channel* MADAGASCAR
Delagoa Bay
L. St Lucia

ATLANTIC OCEAN

INDIAN OCEAN

In the dead of night he paid us a visit alone, and sat down very quietly and mournfully at our fire. Livingstone and I woke up and greeted him, and then he dreamily recounted the history of his life, his wars, escapes, successes and conquests, and the far-distant wandering in his raids. By the fire's glow and flicker among the reeds, with that tall dark earnest speaker and his keenly-attentive listeners, it has always appeared to me one of the most weird scenes I ever saw. With subdued manner and voice Sebituane went on through the live-long night till near the dawn, in low tones only occasionally interrupted by a question from Livingstone. . . .

A fortnight later he was on his deathbed with pneumonia. 'Sebituane will never die', said the witch-doctors; but the chief himself called Livingstone to his side: 'See if I am any longer a man; I am done.' Livingstone's small son Robert was with him. To a servant, Sebituane said: 'Take Robert to Maunku [one of his wives] and tell her to give him some milk.' Those were his last words.

'I never felt so much grieved by the loss of a black man before', Livingstone confessed. 'Alas! alas! Sebituane. I might have said more to him. God forgive me. Free me from blood-guiltiness.' He was face to face with the question of how eternal damnation of the soul of one who dies in total ignorance of the very existence of Christ can be reconciled with the ever-lasting mercy of a God of love who died to save mankind. It was a contradiction that he never resolved. As for Sebituane, 'the deep dark question of what is to become of such as he must be left where we find it, believing that, assuredly, the Judge of all the earth will do right'.

While they were waiting in camp for the permission of Sebituane's heir to proceed on their journey, Livingstone came to a decision that determined the future course of his life. Oswell recorded: 'After we had been lying for some time on the Chobe river he suddenly announced his intention of going down to the west coast. We were about 1,800 miles off it. To my reiterated objection that it would be impossible – "I'm going down, I mean to go down," was the only answer.' Oswell knew by now that it was useless to reiterate objections. His friend was not the easiest of companions, and Oswell had this to say:

One trait in his character was, to do whatever he had set his mind on. In an Englishman we might, I think, have called the phase obstinacy, but with Livingstone it was 'Scottishness'. It was not the *sic volo sic jubea* of imperiousness, but a quiet determination to carry out his own views in his own way, without feeling himself bound to give a reason or explanation further than that he intended to do so-and-so. This was an immense help to him, for it made him supremely self-reliant. . . .

I have sat seven weeks with him on the bank of a swamp, because he was unwilling to run counter to the wishes of the people. I pressed him to move on with the horses; no active opposition would have been offered, but he would not wound the prejudices of the natives – and he was right. With his quiet endurance and entire lack of fussiness and excitability, content to wait and let patience have her perfect work, he was eminently the *justum et tenacum propositi virum* on whom man or elements could make little impression – yet strangely withal very enthusiastic. This nature fitted him for the successful traveller and trustworthy companion. We were the firmest of friends, both a trifle obstinate, but we generally agreed to differ, and in all matters concerning the natives I of course waived my crude opinions to his matured judgement. . . .

He was pre-eminently a *Man* – patient, all-enduring under hardships, content to win his way by inches, but never swerving from it; gentle, kindly, brotherly to the children of the land; absolutely unruffled amidst danger and difficulty, and well satisfied to see but one step in advance. If ever a man carried out the Scriptural injunction to take no thought for the morrow, that man was David Livingstone.

A site for a mission station still had not been found and the two men decided to make a reconnaissance further to the north-east, where the Makololo reported the existence of a wide river. Leaving Mary and the children by the Chobe they pushed on through swampy country, swimming their horses over many streams, for about a hundred and thirty miles through the district of Linyanti, to reach the river on 4 August 1851. The Makololo called it Sesheke at this point, but Livingstone had no doubt that he had been 'rewarded by the discovery of the Zambesi, in the centre of the continent. This was a most important point, for that river was not previously known to exist there at all.' Even at the driest time of year, it was four or five hundred yards wide and flowing deeply; in the wet season, it rose twenty feet to flood an immense wide, flat valley. There was no site here for a permanent mission. But the missionary had already resolved to return alone to make a final search, and to 'open up the interior by a path either to the east or the west coast'. They left the banks of the Chobe on 13 August

1851, and reached Cape Town seven months later, a journey of some fifteen hundred miles.

While proceeding down the Zouga, an event occurred which Oswell described in a letter. His companion seemed determined to camp in a grassless locality for eight days: 'After several fruitless objections from Oswell which elicited the same obstinate reply, "I'm going to stay," I said: "Come, out with it! What's the matter?" "Oh, nothing. . . . Mrs L. had a little son last night." So I waited eight days very willingly, but I had a deal of trouble to get the reason out of him.' The event did not go unrecorded by the father. A single entry in his journal reads: 'September 15th, A son, William Oswell Livingstone, born at a place we always call Bellevue.' He became known as Zouga.

Livingstone had decided to send the whole family back to Britain. There the family, he believed, would be properly cared for, and he expected his Society to help in their support. That he did not make the decision lightly is clear from a letter to his Directors: 'Nothing but a strong conviction that the step will tend to the Glory of Christ would make me orphanise my children. Even now my bowels yearn over them – they will forget me . . . so powerfully convinced am I that it is the will of our Lord I should, *I will go, no matter who opposes*; but from you I expect nothing but encouragement.'

'I will go, no matter who opposes'

Time was strengthening the conviction that 'if God has accepted my service, then my life is charmed till my work is done'. If God withdrew support, then he was no longer following God's purposes and life for him would have no meaning, and 'some simple thing will give me my quietus'. The simplicity of this faith imparted a strength of will that did at times seem superhuman. As for Mary and the children, they were in God's hands and He would look after them. To doubt this would be to doubt divine goodness and mercy. His only doubts were of his own worthiness. 'I would venture anything for Christ', he wrote to his sister. 'Pity I have so little to give.'

His salary was still only £100 a year, and by the start of 1852 it was all spent, and more, on bare necessities. At Kolobeng he had to buy a wagon and supplies to continue to Cape Town, which they reached in March 1852, penniless and almost in rags. But Oswell had gone ahead and placed money at their disposal to enable them to cut a decent figure in this sophisticated colonial capital. He brushed aside their thanks

Livingstone had been away from civilisation for eleven years when he and his family reached Cape Town by ox-wagon in 1852. Only Oswell's generosity enabled them to buy clothes and find lodgings until passages to England could be got for Mary and the four children.

by saying that the money was really Livingstone's because it came from his 'estate' – from the tusks of elephants killed in Bechuanaland. Oswell had, indeed, once gained £100 worth of ivory (four elephants) in a single day.

This was Livingstone's first return to civilisation for eleven years. A flight of stairs was so unfamiliar that he felt inclined to come down backwards, as if on a ladder. At long last he was able to get attention for a swollen uvula that had caused him constant discomfort, sometimes reducing his voice to a painful

croak. He had tried to persuade his father-in-law to cut it out
with a pair of nail-scissors at Kuruman, but Mr Moffat, albeit
a courageous man, had shrunk from the task. After the operation 'the tongue feels as if it needed oiling. . . . I feel dreadfully
at a loss for words in English, while ideas come up in
barrowfuls. . . . What a little thing is sufficient to bring down to
old wifishness such a tough tyke as I consider myself!'

On 23 April 1852, Mary and the four children sailed from
the Cape. 'My heart yearns incessantly after you', he wrote a

Evangelist, geographer, map-maker, naturalist and doctor, this many-sided man was also an accomplished linguist and learnt, and reduced to writing, a number of African dialects. He compiled a vocabulary of the Tswana tongue.

fortnight later. 'I never show my feelings; but I can truly say, my dearest, that I loved you when I married you, and the longer I lived with you, I loved you the better.' While in Cape Town, he took lessons from Thomas Maclear, the Astronomer Royal, who became a fast friend to whom he was to send back a continual flow of observations made during future journeys. He bought what few provisions he could afford and started back for Kolobeng in June 1852.

He never reached it. At Kuruman he was delayed while repairs were carried out to a broken wagon. In this he saw, once again, the hand of God; had it not been for the delay he would have been at Kolobeng when the long-expected Boer

In Cape Town Livingstone took lessons from the Astronomer Royal, Thomas Maclear, in astronomical observation and mapmaking.

raid took place. A large, well-armed commando smashed the place to bits, carried off all the furniture and equipment that was worth having, destroyed books and medicines and attacked Sechele's town, killing sixty of the Bakwena. Livingstone would have been unlikely to survive since the purpose of the raid was to destroy him. As it was, he lost everything he possessed, and remarked with typical stoicism that now he would travel all the lighter and had no need to make a Will. But anger flared up at the wanton destruction: 'If they had made use of my books and medicines I could have forgiven them; but tearing, smashing and burning them was beyond measure galling.' This rankled for the rest of his life. He got no redress, and nor

Livingstone's favourite
Africans were the Makololo,
an offshoot of the Basuto
people who, under their
chief Sebituane, had invaded
Barotseland not long before
Livingstone arrived. This
print depicts a Makololo
dwelling and *al fresco* meal.

did Sechele, whose people had lost all their corn and cattle as
well as their houses and in some cases their lives.

When he left Kuruman in December 1852, with three ox-
drivers, a single wagon and a bare minimum of provisions, he
expected to be away for about two years. It was a hard journey
and, for the lonely European, a time of soul-searching and the
nearest he ever came to doubts. Night after night by the camp-
fire, often plagued by insects, drenched by rain, bleeding from
thorn-gashes, he filled his journal with observations of nature
mingled with inner anxieties. 'Have I seen the end of my wife
and children? – the breaking up of all connections with earth,
leaving this fair and beautiful world, and knowing so little of
it?' And what would happen when the final wrench came? 'My
soul, whither wilt thou emigrate? Where wilt thou lodge the
first night after leaving this body? Will an angel soothe

thy flutterings? for sadly fluttered wilt thou be on entering upon eternity. Oh, if Jesus speak one word of peace, that will establish in thy breast an everlasting calm!' No word came, but faith endured. 'Death is a glorious event to one going to Jesus.' His thoughts turned back continually to his family. 'I think much of my poor children', he wrote.

But at Linyanti, six or seven thousand tribesmen turned out to greet Sebituane's white friend. They had planted a garden for him in the hopes of his return. From the start he loved the 'very confiding and affectionate' Makololo, and continued to do so despite their faults, which included cowardice and lying. Their new chief, Sekelutu, aged eighteen, 'a soft good-natured young man', proved just as anxious as his uncle had been to help the missionary. But soon after his arrival at the chief's headquarters on 23 May 1853, Livingstone succumbed to a severe attack of 'African fever' – amazingly, his first after twelve years in Africa. At first he thought it was merely a cold. But when it worsened he placed himself in the hands of Sekelutu's witch-doctors to see what they could do. After being 'smoked like a red-herring over green twigs' and subjected to various charms, he concluded that European medicine was better; and best of all was a stout heart and refusal to 'lay by'.

As soon as he recovered, he tried to interest the Makololo in his message, but with scant success. 'They listen, but never suppose that the truths must become embodied in actual life.' Less experienced missionaries would have despaired, but as for him, 'our dreams must come true, even though they are no more than dreams. The world is rolling on to a golden age. . . .' But in the short term it appeared to be rolling backwards into darkness, for the slave-trade was even then beginning to thrust its tentacles into Barotseland. The year before, on their first visit to Sebituane's, Livingstone and Oswell had heard that a tribe to the west, the Mambari, who had Portuguese blood, had begun to barter guns for boys – one boy, one gun. 'The Makololo declare that they never heard of people being bought and sold till then, and disliked it, but the desire to possess the guns prevailed.'

This was Livingstone's first contact with the slave-trade then creeping in from both sides of Africa, mainly through the agency of half-caste Portuguese and Arab traders. After his first visit to Linyanti, he wrote to his Directors in London: 'You will see from the accompanying sketch what an immense

region God in His Providence has opened up. If we can enter
in and form a settlement we shall be able in the course of a very
few years to put a stop to the slave trade in that quarter.' So
germinated in his mind the idea which was to become his life's
purpose. This limited objective of 1851, to stop the trade from
spreading along the Zambesi, was to grow into the grand
general aim of exterminating it throughout the whole continent
of Africa.

The question of a site for a mission station further north was
still unsettled. Sekelutu accompanied him on his search and
they set out with a retinue of 160 warriors in full battle attire
and a herd of oxen. They reached the Zambesi and proceeded
in a fleet of thirty-three canoes, propelled by young men stand-

ing upright to wield their paddles with bravura as the Barotse do today. The river was over a mile wide and dotted with forest-clad islands; along its banks were many villages whose inhabitants were skilled workers in wood, iron and pottery; the soil was fertile, crops abundant, God had smiled upon the country; yet the hearts of men were very black. As they proceeded through Barotseland, Livingstone grew more and more depressed by the crude manifestations of savagery he was obliged to witness. Two villagers were seized by Sekelutu's attendants, hacked in pieces before his eyes and thrown into the river merely on suspicion of plotting against the chief. When a buffalo or hippopotamus was killed, the people fell on its raw, still-warm carcass like beasts of prey and devoured it down to the last scrap of offal. Noisy, obscene and pointless dances went on almost without end; quarrels broke out continually; 'to endure the dancing, roaring, and singing, the jesting, anecdotes, grumbling, quarrelling, and murdering of these children of nature, seemed more like a severe penance than anything I had met with . . .'. Malaria is a notoriously depressing sickness and seven severe attacks in nine weeks cast down even his indomitable spirit. 'The more intimately I become acquainted with barbarism, the more disgusting does heathenism become. It is inconceivably vile. . . . They need a healer. May God enable me to be such to them!'

The fever left him emaciated, weak and subject to giddy spells, and again he had failed to find a mission site. 'I thus had a fair excuse of coming home and saying that "the door was shut because the Lord's time had not yet come".' Needless to say, he did no such thing. He returned to Linyanti and recruited twenty-seven volunteers to accompany him into the unknown. 'These men were not hired, but sent to enable me to accomplish an object as much desired by their chief and most of his people as by me. They were eager to obtain free and profitable trade with white men.'

Preparations for a departure which all recognised might be forever in this world were simple. Livingstone gave his journal to Sekelutu with instructions to send it to Moffat at Kuruman if he should fail to return. His wagon and few remaining goods he left with the chief. Then he wrote his farewell letters. To his father:

The conversion of a few, however valuable their souls may be, cannot be put into the scale against the knowledge of truth spread

Feast of the Potamus. Shire March 2nd 1863. CJM

Scenes of savagery witnessed on his
travels depressed and disgusted Livingstone,
especially the butchery of animals, and
feasts on raw flesh that followed.
Although often obliged to shoot to keep his
men in meat, he disliked killing animals
and never did so for sport.

over the whole country. . . . My blessing on my wife. May God comfort her. If my watch comes back after I am cut off, it belongs to Agnes. If my sextant, it is Robert's. The Paris medal to Thomas. Double-barrelled gun to Zouga. – Be a father to the fatherless, and a husband to the widow, for Jesus' sake.

And finally, to Moffat: 'I shall open a path to the interior, or perish.' He left Linyanti on 11 November 1853, with the twenty-seven volunteers, three muskets, a rifle and a double-barrelled shotgun; a few pounds of coffee, tea and sugar, and twenty pounds of beads; a small tent; chronometers; sextant and thermometer; a magic lantern to illustrate his religious talks; and two canisters, one for medicines and a few books, the other for decent clothes to wear if he ever reached Luanda, capital of Angola on the west coast. His reading matter consisted of the Bible, a nautical almanack, a set of logarithm tables and a Sechuana Pentateuch.

Thus ended the first stage of his career, which had spanned twelve years and taken him to the age of forty: that of an itinerant missionary preaching the Gospel to a handful of indifferent Africans. Now it moved into the wider sphere of geographical discovery, made with the sole purpose of opening ways to the interior by which civilisation, bearing Christianity on its back as a snail bears its shell, would advance to save souls and to free their owners from the growing menace of the slave trade. In this next stage of his career he made, in the words of a leading authority, Dr J. W. Gregory, 'the greatest single contribution to African geography which has ever been made'.

Islands inhabited by people
of bad repute among

The chief Nyembwe a ke...
This people have a bad name
unruly and robbers ===
chief Moenge

Kamolondor
I ui the water

Lake

Lualaba

Kinkon...

Rua

Kabuire·

R.L abuli

Iofunzo R.

R Lokinda

ompuato

R. Lyao

Kabwabwata
Kabuire or
R Choma

R. Kamaombue

R. Kibure

chief Kara
R. Luaese

Buire

Moeruenga M[c]s

3000 feet

Kalelle
Karembue

Moero
-okala

Kirwa inlet

Kisumba inlet

R. Kalun...

R. Loretoon...

Iofuk...

Karemba

Jale or Kalungi

Lunda

Forest

Rua

R. Luapula

Lundo

Bausi

R. Luongo

R. Rofuou

Mbor[n]wa

Iramba country

Malipalana
chief Rofumbi

3 Lone Explorer

R. Lotuko

6 hours

raro

Mpara
Browdest
part

bhanza
Thupa

Iopere

Fipa

Zongive
Tende
Supa

manda
chunda
Luamba

Maxeroza

Hot fountain
country

Karembe
Itawa

Msenga
nango

R Ionangwa

Tambala

Iofubu

Karambo

Msama's country

R Iofubu

Iofubu Moe

Loela

Msenga
chombu
chinrem

I. Motongo
I N'komba

Chitimbwa's

R Mulungu

Ulungu

R Aeesy
v Pambere

Ulungu

Siembere

Kosonoo'oo

Karembe

Kakaura

Itawa

chaimba

Baulungu

Lochenge

Mambwe Mt

Iofubu

byue

Chityne

Likwene

Tirola

Chasa
Lobem

Loombe

Upland
Forest

Losanswo ridge

mt amba
mdlembo

Lobemba

Lubunaeno

Loembe

Lokotu

Lokiako

mwabo

moruoke

chibunda

aia

Bemba   or

THEY STARTED IN CANOES, paddling up the broad Zambesi past villages where Sekelutu's friendship assured them of provisions from local chiefs. In return, Livingstone showed his magic lantern slides of biblical scenes, some of which startled his audience. A slide depicting Abraham about to plunge his dagger into Isaac's breast proved particularly alarming. When the slide was moved, the dagger seemed to be coming straight at the spectators, and all the women, crying 'mother! mother!' rushed off 'helter-skelter, tumbling pell-mell over each other, and over the little idol-huts and tobacco bushes; we could not get one of them back again'.

Every morning, the party was away by five to paddle in the cool of the day, and at eleven halted to rest and eat a biscuit with honey. Often Livingstone was too weak from fever to shoot for the pot and in the evening 'coffee again, and a biscuit, or a piece of coarse bread made of maize meal, make up the bill of fare'. Even when he was well enough to shoot, he sometimes could not bring himself to destroy the graceful animals, but merely lay and looked at them until his men came up and scared them away. 'If we had been starving I could have slaughtered them with as little hesitation as I should cut off a patient's leg; but I felt a doubt, and the antelope got the better of it.'

Attacks of malaria were severe and frequent. 'In the cold stage I vomit all matters contained in the stomach. In the sweating stage . . . the ugly phantoms which are often seen in continued fever appear and prevent sleep. I awake in the morning exhausted and wet with perspiration. No appetite, and a feeling of great lassitude and disinclination to speak.' Yet through it all he led his Makololo forward, negotiated with village headmen who became less friendly the further they proceeded, and filled his notebooks with detailed observations of plants and animals, geology and the habits of the native tribes. He described thirty unfamiliar varieties of bird and was the first to identify a species of plover that cleans crocodiles' teeth by pecking in their open jaws. Whenever he was able, he took bearings by the moon and stars, fixed the latitude and longitude, and drew sketch-maps with an accuracy which was to astonish geographers of the outside world.

It had been generally assumed, until this journey, that the Kalahari Desert continued northwards to become one with the Sahara. Livingstone was the first European to find that, on the

PREVIOUS PAGES Livingstone won the warmest admiration of Thomas Maclear, the Astronomer Royal, who said that what he had done was unprecedented; anyone could have followed his path across Africa, using his sketch-maps, and be sure of his own position.

contrary, north of the Kalahari lay a great network of water-ways and a soil so fertile that it would, he believed, 'yield grain sufficient to feed vast multitudes'. This land was rich in cattle, game and ivory, and in people anxious for trade. It was also beautiful. The upper Zambesi (now in Zambia) wound through 'charming meadows' full of flowers, with 'bees to sip their nectar', amid trees 'covered with a profusion of the freshest foliage'. The whole gave an impression of a gentle-man's carefully-tended park.

As they travelled northwards, it grew wetter and the going heavier. Continuous rain held them up for days at a time, their clothes were always soaked and they could find nowhere dry to pitch camp. They had reached the fringes of the great rain-forests of Central Africa still unknown to geographers, yet already there was a diffusion of European goods. One of the Makololo picked up a bit of steel watch-chain made in England, and Mambari traders were exchanging slaves for Manchester cottons 'so wonderful that the Makololo could not believe them to be the work of mortal hands'. They thought the cotton prints came out of a lake, and beads were washed up on the shore. When Livingstone tried to explain about machinery they exclaimed: 'Truly, ye are gods!'

'Truly, ye are gods!'

In the forests, food grew short and by January 1854, they were reduced to a few unpalatable roots of cassava, raw fungi and small rodents, including 'a light blue mole'. The Makololo had to hack a way with axes through thick, drip-ping undergrowth that might conceal suspicious tribesmen armed with poisoned arrows. Here Livingstone first came upon a sight that was to become only too familiar in years ahead. Beside the camp of two half-caste Portuguese traders, a gang of newly-purchased young women were hoeing the ground – in chains.

These central African kingdoms deep in the forest, with their idols and stockaded villages, were quite different from anything Livingstone had seen in the south. One dignified chief received him seated on a leopard-skin throne, dressed in a scarlet and green baize jacket and an elaborate bead and feather head-dress; around him were about a thousand armed tribesmen, and at his side between one and two hundred wives. No one had seen a white man before and the poverty of this traveller, his small number of attendants and his lack of goods must have been sorely puzzling. Even half-caste traders marched with

Once into the central African jungle, he and his companions had to hack a way by compass bearings through vegetation so dense they could not see five yards ahead, and could sometimes only travel two or three miles a day.

drums, trumpets and armed guards. The chief kept them there for ten days and then presented Livingstone with a ten-year-old girl. He could not understand why his visitor refused this gift, and produced a larger girl, assuming that the first had been rejected as too small. Finally he provided guides, food and extra men to carry four elephant tusks of Sekelutu's which Livingstone was taking to the coast 'to test the market'.

They were travelling now on foot or, in Livingstone's case, on the back of his riding-ox Sinbad. Rain continued unabated, their gunpowder was sodden, the scientific instruments rusty, their clothes mildewed. When they came to a great waterlogged plain linking the Zambesi with the Congo river systems, they waded through 'millions of acres of fine hay', and at night bivouacked on low mounds a few feet above it. When they reached Lake Diolo, the leader was too weak from continual bouts of malaria to examine it; he had eaten nothing for two days and could scarcely sit on the ox.

The closer they approached to civilisation, in the shape of Portuguese trading posts, the harder it became to get food; the people demanded payment, and Livingstone's party had little left to offer. A few beads or bangles, a tattered shirt, a razor – these were spurned; it must be 'a man, a gun or an ox'. Nothing would convince the tribesmen that the Makololo were not Livingstone's slaves. In the country of the Chiboque, the expedition nearly foundered. To the usual request, its leader 'declared that we were all ready to die rather than give up one of our number to be a slave; my men might as well give me as I give one of them, for we were all free men'. Angry Chiboque, brandishing muskets, surrounded the little party and one of them 'made a charge at my head from behind, but I quickly brought round the muzzle of my gun to his mouth, and he retreated. . . . I then sat silent for some time. It was rather trying for me, as I knew that the Chiboque would aim at the white man first; but I was careful not to appear flurried, and, having four barrels ready for instant action, looked quietly at the savage scene around.' This formidable coolness nonplussed tribesmen accustomed to dealing with slave-traders who showed little fight. It was typical of Livingstone's detachment that he quite saw their point: 'They had been accustomed to get a slave or two from every trader who passed them, and now that we disputed the right, they viewed the infringement of what they considered lawfully due, with the most virtuous indignation.'

To avoid such demands, they left the route followed by slavers to find a new way of their own further north, through boggy country flooded by swollen streams. Livingstone was again prostrated by fever, sometimes in a coma. Even Sinbad rebelled. They were marching in pouring rain through 'many miles of gloomy forest in gloomier silence', expecting to be attacked at any moment, the leader 'too ill to care much whether we were attacked or not', and trying unsuccessfully to dodge the creepers which festooned the trees, when, without warning, Sinbad bolted, threw his rider on to his head and kicked him viciously on the thigh. 'I felt none the worse for this rough treatment, but would not recommend it to others as a palliative in cases of fever.' Continual fever had reduced him almost to a skeleton, and his skin, tightly stretched over the projecting bones, was chafed raw by friction from Sinbad's back. At this nadir of his fortunes, the Makololo, not surprisingly, announced that they were turning back. In that case, replied their leader, he would continue alone; and he

OVERLEAF Thomas Baines made the first paintings of the Victoria Falls in 1862. Animals pursued by lions sometimes plunged over the lip of the chasm into which the waters cascaded.

ABOVE Livingstone's
exploration of the Zambesi
valley coincided with an
expansion of the slave trade.
On the West coast, half-caste
Portuguese traders were
still buying and marching
slaves to the coast for
shipment, as shown here,
mainly to the West Indies
and America, despite the
illegality of the trade.

retired into the remnants of his tent to pray and to record in his journal: 'O Almighty God, help, help! and leave not this wretched people to the slave-dealer and Satan.' After a day of indecision, one of the Makololo poked his head through the tent to say: 'We will never leave you. Wherever you lead, we will follow.' 'They are all right again', their leader wrote, 'and I thank God for it.'

Less than a week later, they emerged from the forest to see below a broad, sunlit, beautiful valley which reminded Livingstone of the vale of the Clyde. It was on a much larger scale, however; a hundred miles broad, with the River Cuango at the bottom. Livingstone was so weak he had to be held up by his companions, much to his chagrin: 'I never liked to see a man, either sick or well, giving in effeminately.'

The local tribesmen refused to sell them food 'for the poor old ornaments my men had to offer. . . . Everything was gone except my instruments.' When, almost starving, they killed one of their few remaining oxen, the angry tribesmen demanded a share. 'You may as well give it', they told the Makololo, 'for we shall take all after we have killed you tomorrow.' So the destitute party crept away before dawn in a heavy downpour, and six hours' march brought them to the bank of the Cuango river which marked the eastern extremity of Portuguese domains.

But how to cross it? The riparian chief demanded, as usual, payment of a man. Livingstone's blanket, all he had, was angrily refused. In this predicament, a young half-caste sergeant of militia appeared. Despite musket fire from the angry chief's men, he got the destitute party safely across the river to Portuguese-held territory, and 'all our difficulties with the border tribes were at an end'.

It was one of the ironies of Livingstone's career that the people who most befriended him were those he was striving to destroy. Later, Arab slavers were to aid and succour him and on more than one occasion to save his life. The Portuguese paid lip-service to the abolitionist cause but winked at the practice of slavery, and a large class of half-breeds thrived on its profits. But no one could have treated this foreign anti-slavery crusader with greater generosity than the Portuguese. The sergeant of militia, Cypriano, took him and his bedraggled men to his house, feasted them all and placed before the leader a 'magnificent breakfast'. Meals were 'partaken of with decency and good manners', everything was clean and tidy; Cypriano could read and write, and owned books on medicine and an encyclopaedia. While rain held them up, he 'bared his garden' for them without a hint of payment. Even in this attenuated form, civilisation seemed infinitely preferable to savagery.

Three days' hard march through wet grass towering two feet above their heads brought them, on 13 April 1854, to Cassenge, the easternmost Portuguese station in Angola. The Commandant's welcome was every bit as warm as his sergeant's. This lone white man wandering in from the east must have seemed an odd fish to the Portuguese. What sort of a missionary was he, they inquired, who took bearings on the stars, was a doctor of medicine and had a wife and four children – and a moustache? What was his true rank in the British army? On his side, he was very favourably impressed by his hosts' lack of colour prejudice – blacks 'sit at the tables of the richest men in the country' – by their humane treatment of their half-caste children and by their civilised behaviour. 'Nowhere else in Africa is there so much goodwill between Europeans and natives', he concluded.

At Cassenge, Livingstone sold Sekelutu's tusks which, faithful to his promise, he had managed to transport. He obtained a highly satisfactory price – one tusk produced enough calico to pay their way down to the coast, still three hundred miles away. All the merchants of Cassenge, carried in hammocks by slaves, saw the party off on its last lap. Its leader would 'never forget their disinterested kindness'. This even thawed a little of his ingrained austerity. The Commandant at Ambaca recommended wine as an antidote to fever and he took his first glass for thirty years. Fever had reduced him to a point at which 'I forget the days of the week, the names of those about me and think, had I been asked, I could not have told my own.' On the last stage of the journey, he suffered so horribly from dysentery that he could not stay on Sinbad's back for more than ten minutes at a time.

On 31 May 1854, they saw the sea. The Makololo were overwhelmed. 'We marched along with our leader believing that what the ancients had always told us was true, that the world has no end; but all at once the world said to us, "I am finished, there is no more of me!" They had always imagined that the world was one extended plain.' As they approached Luanda, Livingstone was seized with panic. 'In a population of twelve thousand souls, there was but one genuine English gentleman'; would he be friendly, or 'one of those crusty mortals one would rather not meet at all?' He need not have worried. The English gentleman was Edmund Gabriel, British Commissioner for the suppression of the slave trade. Mr Gabriel made him welcome and nursed him with devotion through a combined onslaught of dysentery and malaria which would almost certainly have killed him had not three British cruisers dropped anchor in the harbour, one with a naval surgeon on board. The drugs prescribed by Mr Cockin of the *Polyphemus*, combined with Mr Gabriel's nursing, pulled him through.

As soon as he was well enough, he called on the acting Governor, and found him a most intelligent, congenial and benign bishop; but the splendid celebration of the Feast of Corpus Christi in the Cathedral aroused his Protestant distaste. He took the Makololo to see it – they had been fitted out with striped cotton robes and red caps by Mr Gabriel – and overheard them saying 'they had seen the white men charming their demons', the same phrase they had used to describe the pagan rites of the Batonga on the Zambesi.

Soon after Livingstone reached Luanda, capital of Angola, three British cruisers on an anti-slavery patrol dropped anchor in the harbour. Among the ships' officers he made friends with was Lieutenant Norman Bedingfeld RN, who subsequently joined his Expedition of 1858-63.

The British cruisers were another matter. The Makololo were at first apprehensive, having been told that on arrival at the coast they would be killed and eaten. Their fears vanished when they got on board and soon they were sharing beef and bread with the sailors and firing off a cannon. 'It is not a canoe at all, it is a town', they exclaimed. Luanda was altogether to their liking. They made so much money by trading in firewood and unloading coal that twenty porters – provided by the Bishop – were hired for the return journey to carry all the goods they had acquired.

The 'exhilarating presence' of the ships' officers delighted Livingstone, especially as their task was to blockade the port against slave-trading vessels. He made particular friends with Lieutenant Norman Bedingfeld, whom he subsequently invited to join his expedition of 1858-63. The sailors made him a new tent. The Captain of the *Polyphemus* offered him a free passage to England and pressed him to accept, and the temptation to re-join his wife and children was great. Nevertheless, he refused.

I had brought a party of Sekelutu's people with me, and found the tribes near the Portuguese settlements so very unfriendly, that it would be altogether impossible for my men to return alone. I therefore resolved to decline the tempting offers of my naval friends, and take back my Makololo companions to their chief, with a view of trying to make a path from his country to the east coast by means of the great river Zambesi.

This decision must have been all the harder to make because there had been a sad disappointment at Luanda: no letters from Mary; and although he put off his departure for a month in the hope of hearing from her, nothing arrived. When he could delay no longer, the Portuguese merchants presented each of his men with a suit of clothing, provided a horse (which died *en route*) and a complete colonel's uniform for Sekelutu, and added two donkeys. He himself bought muskets, plenty of cloth and a collection of plants and seeds to introduce into Barotseland. After handing over letters, dispatches, maps and part of his journal for conveyance to England, he left for Linyanti on 20 September 1854.

Livingstone was astonished by the fertility of the soil and the industry of the people of Angola. Every woman, as she walked along carrying a hoe, a clay pot and a baby, had also in her hand a spindle and spun the cotton as she went. With remarkable scientific accuracy, he noted, almost every day and however ill, the birds, beasts, insects, reptiles, plants and geology of every hill and valley that he passed, as well as the customs and behaviour of the inhabitants. Of a fallen baobab tree: 'The concentric rings seem to possess each a distinct vitality, hence when the bark is stripped off it only exposes a new living bark to the air. The end of the tree shewed each concentric ring growing out from the cut surface, appearing in *relievo* and enabling one to count with ease 85 rings in one semi diameter of 5 spans.' 'An insect burrows into the orange trees, discharging a yellow dust constantly, and soon kills them if not prevented by the very simple expedient of thrusting a thorn very firmly into the burrow and cutting it off close to the bark.'

While on the march, he would pause to improvise experiments, such as this concerning an insect of the family *Cercopidae* which distilled a clear liquid from certain trees:

Finding a colony of these insects busily distilling on a branch of the *Ricinus communis*, or castor-oil plant, I denuded about 20 inches of the bark on the tree side of the insects, and scraped away the inner bark, so as to destroy all the ascending vessels. I also cut a hole in the side of the branch, reaching to the middle, and then cut out the pith and internal vessels. The distillation was then going on at the rate of one drop each 67 seconds, or about 2 ounces $5\frac{1}{2}$ drams in every 24 hours. Next morning the distillation, so far from being affected by the attempt to stop the supplies, supposing they had come up through the branch from the tree, was increased to a drop of every 5 seconds, or 12 drops per minute, making 1 pint (16 ounces) in every 24 hours. . . .

The experiment continued until he cut off the branch, when the insects 'immediately decamped, as insects will do from either a dead branch or a dead animal, which Indian hunters soon know, when they sit down on a recently killed bear'. He concluded that the insects drew moisture not from the sap but from the atmosphere, and possessed a power, not yet understood, to sustain 'life-long action without fatigue'.

Of his observations of moon and stars, the Astronomer Royal at the Cape, Thomas Maclear, had this to say: 'I never knew a man who, knowing scarcely anything of the method of making geographical observations, or laying down positions,

St Paul de Loanda (Luanda), where Livingstone recovered his health as a guest of the Portuguese; from a sketch by Captain Henry Need.

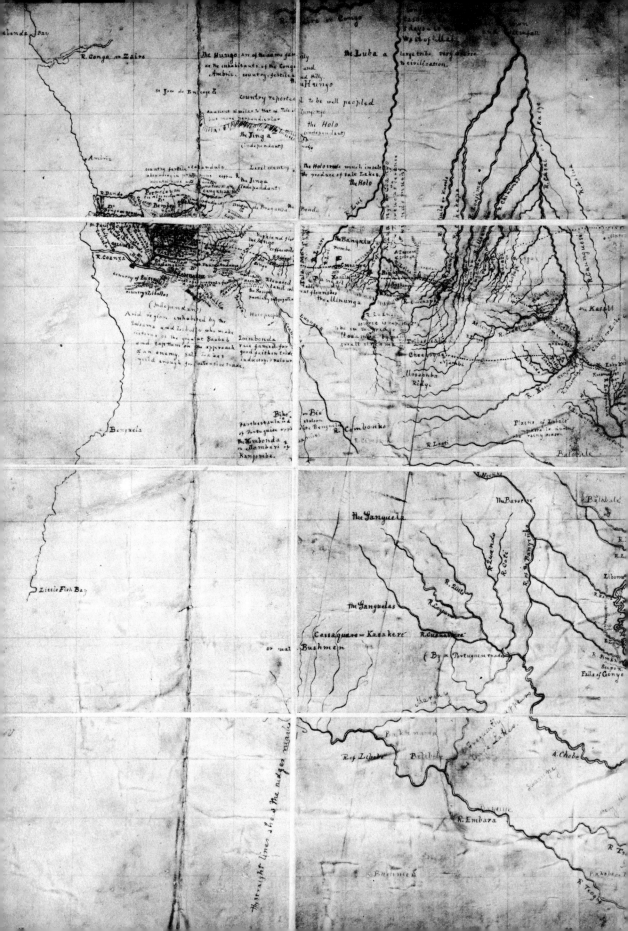

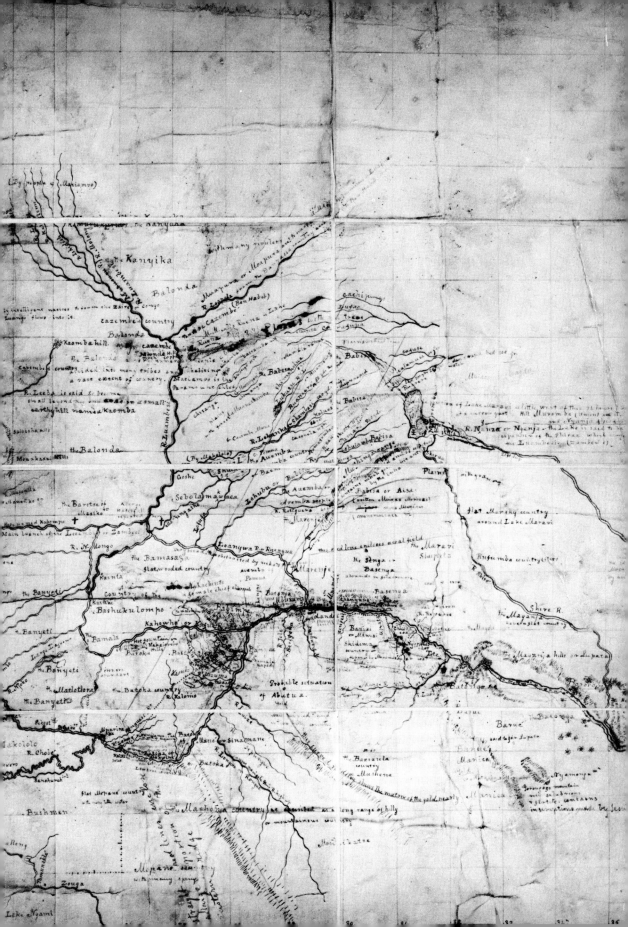

PREVIOUS PAGES In Angola
and the unknown central
regions, Livingstone made the
first detailed maps of the
intricate river systems of the
region. He discovered that
the central watershed was
not a range of high
mountains but an extensive
plain, giving rise to the
headwaters of the Congo
and the Zambesi.

became so soon an adept that he could take complete lunar
observations, and altitude for time, within fifteen minutes. His
observations of the course of the Zambesi . . . are the finest
specimens of geographical observation I ever met with. 'He went
on to instance the laborious nature of these observations – 2,812
separate readings to fix a single position. 'I say', Maclear
added, 'that what this man has done is unprecedented. You
could go to any point across the entire continent, along
Livingstone's track, and feel certain of your position.' In the
hope of catching a glimpse of the moon, Livingstone remained
for four nights on the banks of the Cuango, sleeping in snatches
and devoured by mosquitoes, only to be disappointed – the
moon never appeared.

While staying with the richest merchant in Angola, Colonel
Pires, news came of a disaster: all his maps, dispatches, letters
and parts of his journal had been lost in the *Forerunner* which
sank with all hands save one off Madeira. But Livingstone 'felt
so glad' that his friend Lieutenant Bedingfeld had not been on
board that he was 'at once reconciled to the labour of re-
writing'. How onerous this labour was, only those who have
experienced it can appreciate: Carlyle, for instance, who re-
wrote the first volume of his *French Revolution*, and T.E.
Lawrence, who did the same for *The Seven Pillars of Wisdom*.
Fortunately Livingstone had kept the notebooks filled with
rough jottings from which he wrote up his journal as he went
along.

He stayed with Colonel Pires, busy with this task, until the
end of 1854, and then set out again up the Cuango valley. It
rained incessantly. Surly chiefs were again obstructive, but
less so than on the outward journey. 'We have now passed two
chiefs who plagued us much when going down, but now were
quite friendly. . . . The alteration in this gentleman's conduct –
the Peace Society would not credit it – is attributable solely to
my people possessing guns.'

Six months after leaving Luanda, Livingstone succumbed to
a severe attack of rheumatic fever brought on by crossing 'an
extensive plain covered with water' on which they made
mounds of mud, like graves, to sleep on. For eight days he 'lay
by' in great pain, until a native trader with whom they had
been travelling, Senhor Pasqual, caught up and applied leeches
to the head and loins, which eased the pain. While still scarcely
fit for travel, his little party was attacked by a band of armed

villagers. One of the naval officers had given him a six-barrelled revolver. 'Taking this in my hand, and forgetting fever, I staggered quickly along the path with two or three of my men, and fortunately encountered the chief. The sight of six barrels gaping into his stomach, with my own ghastly visage looking daggers into his face, seemed to produce an instant revolution in his martial feelings. . . .' After an exchange of threats, remarking 'Tell him to observe that I am not afraid of him', Livingstone calmly mounted Sinbad, turned his back and rode slowly away. 'There was not much danger in the fire that was opened at first, there being so many trees.' By some miracle, no one was wounded, the villagers eventually withdrew and Livingstone, who must have been half-dead from prolonged fever, vomiting of blood, pain and starvation, continued on his way – only to be almost blinded by a blow from a branch, which inflamed the cornea. Despite this, plus renewed hunger and his twenty-seventh bout of fever, in May he sent Maclear an elaborate map of the Cuango river with many sheets of trigonometrical calculations.

'I sit on my ox and think', he wrote to Edmund Gabriel, 'till the sun permits neither thinking nor travelling. I could never keep an umbrella up without risk of a tumble. Sinbad has the same aversion to my reading *Punch*.' He thought about many things – including the riddle of the rivers; where they rose, and why they flowed sometimes in one direction and sometimes in another, with no apparent watershed. Where were the lofty mountains that had been assumed to lie somewhere in the heart of Africa and give birth to rivers as mighty as the Congo, the Zambesi and, above all, the Nile?

As they approached Lake Dilolo, in June 1855, the truth that had been gradually forming in his mind took final shape. This little lake, surrounded by a level plain, 'by giving a portion to the Kasai and another to the Zambesi, distributes its waters to the Atlantic and Indian Oceans'. So here, after all, was the watershed: not a mountain but a plain, only about four thousand feet above sea-level, where one might travel for a month and see nothing higher than an ant-hill or a stunted tree, more or less surrounded by gently-sloping ridges only about a thousand feet higher than the plain.

This discovery, of the first geographical importance, must have seemed to make the whole enterprise worth-while. 'I was not then aware', he wrote, 'that anyone else had discovered

'I sit on my ox and think. . . .'

OVERLEAF The Kebrabasa rapids above Tete on the Zambesi, by Thomas Baines. The rapids destroyed any hopes of navigating vessels up to the Victoria Falls, using the river to carry Christianity and legitimate commerce into the interior.

the elevated trough form of the centre of Africa'; indeed, how could anyone else have done so, since he was the first geographer to see it? Not until he reached Linyanti did he learn that a geographer who had never set foot in Africa had forestalled him. Sir Roderick Murchison had reached the same conclusion by studying old maps and reports, and advanced it as a theory to a meeting of the Royal Geographical Society in 1852. Livingstone admitted to a feeling of 'considerable chagrin' – due, he told himself, to pride. He overcame it, and became a devoted admirer of his fellow-Scot, whom he was in time to describe as 'the best friend I ever had'.

Meanwhile, weak as he was, Lake Dilolo delighted him. 'The sight of the blue waters, and the waves lashing the shore, had a most soothing influence on the mind after so much lifeless, flat, and gloomy forest.' The Hebridean in him still yearned for 'the grand old ocean – that has life in it; but the flat uniformity over which we had roamed made me feel as if buried alive'.

Once back in the Zambesi valley, old acquaintances greeted and feasted them and treated them as heroes. But they were also back among tsetse-flies, and although a man carrying a branch followed Sinbad everywhere, the ox was bitten, and his doom sealed. Livingstone had never become quite reconciled to Sinbad's crusty temper, streak of vindictiveness and aversion to *Punch*, any more than the ox had become 'reconciled to our perversity, in forcing him away each morning from the pleasant pasturage on which he had fed'. Somewhat heartlessly, he proposed to kill and eat his mount. His men intervened, and took Sinbad along with them to die in his own time from the infection.

As they advanced through Barotseland, their welcome became more and more excited. Chiefs slaughtered oxen, women sang and danced and the headman Pitsane (an arrant coward, according to his master) declaimed their odyssey in lengthy orations. Livingstone held thanksgiving services to which everyone came. The Makololo put on their white European suits – crumpled, one must assume – and red caps, which they had somehow managed to keep intact, and cut a very dashing figure. But they met with a problem: many of their wives, assuming their husbands to be dead, had remarried. Livingstone delivered a Solomon-like judgment: those with only one wife must get her back, but those with several – who did not seem to mind much anyway – must accept the situation. To return all twenty-seven of his men to their homes was one of his most remarkable achievements. They had suffered, as he had, from frequent and often severe illnesses and injuries, but his doctoring, care and imperturbable courage had pulled them through.

On 10 September 1855, almost a year after leaving Luanda, they reached Linyanti. Here they found provisions, mail and newspapers – eighteen months old – sent by Moffat, news of a Gold Medal from the Royal Geographical Society and a eulogy from Thomas Maclear: 'I do not hesitate to assert that no explorer on record has determined his path with the precision you have accomplished. . . . You have accomplished more for the happiness of mankind than has been done by all the African travellers hitherto put together.' There was one bitter blow: no letters from Mary. What became of all she must have written during those two years remains a mystery.

'You have accomplished more for the happiness of mankind. . . .'

There was a great homecoming. Sekelutu donned his colonel's uniform, Pitsane recounted how they had reached the end of the world, and presents from the merchants of Luanda were displayed to demonstrate the promise of trade with the west coast. Sekelutu at once arranged with an Arab to take a party to Luanda carrying ivory for sale. This was not the only Arab at Linyanti; they were beginning to appear in greater numbers as the slave-trade extended its range. One, called Rya Syde, suggested to Livingstone that they should join forces and go to Zanzibar by way of Lake Tanganyika. This had not yet been visited by any European. 'In the event of my going with Rya Syde I would have it in my power to discover Tanganyika or Lake Nyasa, but down the Zambesi seems more in accordance with what I set before my mind on the path of duty.' He added that he would not change his plans 'for the sake of the fame of discovering another Lake, if the Makololo prefer my making the attempt to open a path by water to the East Coast'. So another temptation was put behind him and it was left to Burton and Speke to win the fame three years later.

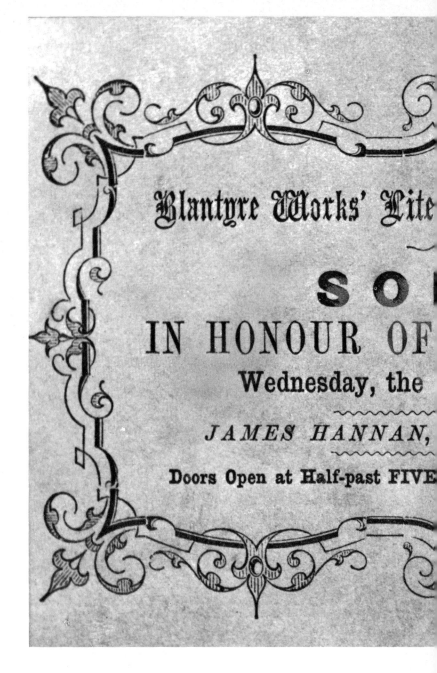

Blantyre Works' Lite

SO

IN HONOUR OF

Wednesday, the

JAMES HANNAN,

Doors Open at Half-past FIVE

4 Privation to Prosperity

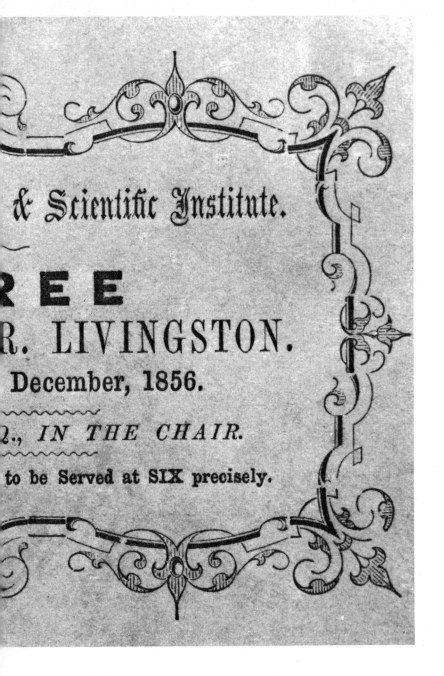

& Scientific Institute.

REE

R. LIVINGSTON.

December, 1856.

., *IN THE CHAIR.*

to be Served at SIX precisely.

A MUCH LARGER PARTY than before – 114 volunteers under a reliable headman, Sekwebu – left Linyanti on 3 November 1855, for the east coast. Sekelutu came with them with his bevy of attendants, a herd of oxen and generous parting presents – beads and hoes for currency, fresh butter, honey, fifteen oxen and twenty-one tusks. These, Sekelutu insisted, were for his white friend's use at the coast to buy anything he fancied. He may have had a guilty conscience: during the friend's absence, he had been raiding his neighbours without provocation, probably for slaves. Livingstone intended to spend the proceeds of the ivory in England on things useful to the chief's people, ranging from newly-invented American bullets designed to kill whales, which he thought would do just as well against elephants, to blue naval caps, a selection of livestock and 'gowns for wives'.

They paddled in great style down the Chobe to the Zambesi and on towards the great Falls, Mosi-oa-tunya, of which both chief and missionary had often heard but which neither had visited. On 17 November they approached the Falls in light canoes at a speed which made even Livingstone feel 'a little tremor'. Disembarking on an island at the lip of the Falls, he lay face-downwards, overwhelmed at the majesty of the sight, the deafening roar of waters hurling themselves into a fissure only eighty feet wide, the leaping clouds of spray, iridescent with rainbows, condensing in vapour over the lush vegetation – 'the most wonderful sight I had witnessed in Africa'. No European before him, he believed, had seen it, though 'scenes so lovely must have been gazed upon by angels in their flight'. (Subsequently he learned that two men with European names had passed by the Falls, but they were not in the full sense Europeans, having been either half-caste Portuguese or native traders who used Portuguese names – a not uncommon practice, as with Senhor Pasqual.) He named the Falls after his Queen – Victoria, 'the only English name I have affixed to any part of the country'.

Having feasted his eyes on their beauties, he set about taking measurements. But his line broke, he had forgotten how to measure a river with a sextant and his estimates turned out later to be much too low. He thought the river above the Falls was a thousand yards wide, whereas it is actually nineteen hundred yards, and the fall about a hundred feet, instead of between two hundred feet at one side and 350 feet at the other.

Next day he planted a little garden on the island, a hundred peach and apricot stones and some coffee beans, and left instructions for its protection against hippopotamuses. Then he carved his initials on a tree – the only occasion on which he 'indulged in this piece of vanity'. Three days later he parted from Sekelutu and set off north-eastwards along a tributary of the Zambesi. He had over six hundred miles to go to Tete, the most westerly Portuguese garrison in Mozambique, and another three hundred to the coast at Quilemane.

This was an easier march than the westward one, and less depressing. There was better food, and more of it. Livingstone had brought wheat flour to bake bread, and took more care to build proper shelters at night. Moreover the climate was healthier and re-awakened hopes that here at last might be found that elusive mission site. He filled his journal with natural history notes and listed over fifty herbal remedies used by witch-doctors – the first of such medical collections made in Africa. Memories of his native land came often to his mind. A black soldier ant stung its termite victims and threw them aside, in a state of coma, 'in the same off-hand style farmers' boys cut off the tops and toss on one side turnips in a field'. A drab-coloured cricket emitted a sound with 'as little modulation as the drone of a Scottish bagpipe'. After passing through what he described as a perfect paradise (now part of Rhodesia), swarming with game, they reached the country of the Batonga, a tribe to which many of his own men belonged.

The Batonga went about stark naked and their method of salutation was to throw themselves to the ground and roll about from side to side yelling loudly and slapping their thighs. Fifteen years' immersion in primitive African customs had not dispelled the prudery created in childhood in that single tenement room as the essential safeguard to human dignity. He found the sight of 'great he-animals all about your camp' most disagreeable, and suggested to a large, fine-bodied old Batonga man that something in the nature of a fig-leaf was desirable. The man looked at him with a 'pitying leer' and roared with laughter. The traveller explained that on his return journey he hoped to have his wife and children with him; such sights must not offend their eyes. 'We have no clothes', the old man pointed out, 'what shall we put on?' A bunch of grass, the missionary suggested. This was a better joke than ever. While Livingstone realised that his scruples seemed ridiculous to the

Batonga, their attitude still baffled him. 'Shame has un-accountably been left out of the question', he wrote plaintively to James Young. 'Can you explain why Adam's first feeling has no trace of existence in his offspring?'

With over a hundred men to feed, the leader had to use his rifle despite his reluctance, and one day shot a male elephant. Next day he watched a female frolic with her calf, unconscious of her human enemies a mile or two away. They played together in a mud-bath, flapping ears and frisking trunks in spontaneous enjoyment of life. All at once, the hunters rushed towards their prey, shouting and blowing on wooden pipes. The cow tried to drive off her attackers but soon she was red with blood from hurled spears, her desperate short charges were futile and she sank down to die. There was no mercy for the calf either. The sight made Livingstone feel sick, even though he had himself killed an elephant the day before. He recognised the element of hypocrisy: 'We ought perhaps to judge acts more leniently to which we have no temptation ourselves.'

After fording the Kafue, they crossed a plain where he saw game in greater quantities than ever before, and all the animals

To greet a visitor, the Batonga, who went about stark naked, threw themselves to the ground and rolled from side to side, The Batonga roared with laughter when Livingstone suggested that a bunch of grass might be worn.

87

so tame, from elephants and buffalo to wart-hogs and kudu. The local tribesmen had not yet acquired guns. Livingstone did not remark on the irony that guns and the civilisation for which he was blazing a trail went together, but his sadness is in his writing. The introduction of God's word was to presage the destruction of God's creatures.

At the start of 1856 they were back on the Zambesi, and felt again the baleful influence of the slave-trade. An Italian slaver had been raiding up the river. The tribesmen were hostile and, for the first time since leaving Sekelutu's, armed. Warriors gathered in large numbers near their camp by the confluence of the Zambesi and the Luangwa rivers, clearly intending to attack as they started to cross. Nearby were the ruins of an old church, with a cross and a broken bell. This evidence of a bygone failure of the faith, combined with the menacing behaviour of the tribesmen, brought on one of Livingstone's moods of gloom:

'Leave me not, forsake me not'

O Jesus, grant me resignation to thy will, & entire reliance on thy powerful hand. On thy work alone I lean. But will thou permit me to plead for Africa? The cause is thine. What an impulse will be given to the idea that Africa is not open if I perish now. See, O Lord, how the heathen rise up against me as they did to thy Son. I commit my way unto thee. . . . A guilty, weak, and helpless worm on thy kind arms I fall. Leave me not, forsake me not. I cast myself and all my cares down at thy feet. Thou knowest all I need, for time and for eternity.

It seems a pity that the important facts about the two healthy longitudinal ridges should not become known in Christendom. Thy will be done.

But in the evening he found consolation, as always, in the Gospels and in particular in Jesus's promise:

And lo, I am with you always, even unto the end of the world. It's the word of a gentleman of the most sacred and strictest honour, and there's an end on't. I will not cross furtively by night as intended. It would appear as flight, and should such a man as I flee? Nay, verily. I shall take observations for lat. & long. tonight, although they may be the last. I feel quite calm now, thank God.

Next morning the situation was even more tense. Armed tribesmen stood round while goods, cattle and men were embarked in batches in the single canoe they had managed to get hold of, and ferried to an island in the middle of the

88

Luangwa river. The leader, last to embark, distracted the warriors' attention by showing them his watch, burning lens and other novelties. It was touch and go until he stepped into the canoe. Then the tension eased, he thanked the warriors for their kindness and gave them presents, and the crisis was over. Once again his unshaken nerve, resolution and restraint had brought them safely through without bloodshed.

They had been travelling hitherto along the north bank of the river, but after passing the abandoned Portuguese settlement of Zumbo, they were advised to cross to the south bank, where the route to Tete was shorter and easier. As it turned out, this crossing was to prove a disaster. When they reached Tete, Livingstone was told that in the district of Chicova there was a 'small rapid' called Kebrabasa (Quebrabasa). Had he known of this at the time, he would certainly have turned aside to examine it, and the false premise on which the Expedition of 1858-63 was based – the navigability of the Zambesi above Tete – would never have been made.

By now their provisions had run out and all the oxen were dead. They foraged in the bush for roots and honey and went hungry to bed. Yet Livingstone's entries in his journal were remarkably cheerful, perhaps because he was free from fever – which he attributed to eating wheaten bread. Nature seemed to be rejoicing, and he rejoiced with it. 'They have nightingales in England, but of all the birds in the world commend me to the merry midnight frogs.' Humming insects, 'brimful of enjoyment', worked away in untold millions to spread 'a mantle of happy existence encircling the world'. Eight miles from Tete, too exhausted to go further, he sent ahead a letter to the Commandant. At three o'clock in the morning, he was woken by a party of soldiers sent by the Commandant, Major Secard, with the 'materials of a substantial breakfast' and a hammock. Revived by the breakfast, he spurned the hammock and marched into Tete on 2 March 1856, to be greeted by the good news of the fall of Sebastopol, which meant that his friend Colonel Steele would no longer be in danger.

Portuguese hospitality in Angola was matched by that in Mozambique. Major Secard placed his house and board at Livingstone's disposal, provided a canoe for the final stage of the journey to Quilemane and settled the Makololo at Tete where he gave them land to cultivate, new clothing and permission to hunt elephants until their leader should return.

Livingstone's fever recurred, his spleen and stomach swelled enormously and once again Portuguese kindness probably saved his life. A trader took him aboard a large sailing launch in whose comfortable cabin the mosquitoes, which were 'something frightful', could be kept at bay. Not so the bats; and, ill as he was, he carried out another experiment. He bared his leg

The first Portuguese settlement Livingstone reached in going down the Zambesi was Tete, about three hundred miles from the coast.

to offer them 'a fair opportunity of playing the vampyre, but they did nothing'.

On 20 May 1856, almost four years to the day after leaving Cape Town, he arrived at Quilemane, to lodge with yet another hospitable Portuguese, Colonel Nunes. There was mail from home awaiting him, but still no word from Mary.

His reflections while waiting for the vessel which the Royal Navy was sending to fetch him were sober and without a trace of self-praise. To open a 'prospect for the elevation of the inhabitants' was exploration's whole aim. 'It does not look as if I reached the goal.' It was at Quilemane that he recorded his famous conclusion: 'I view the end of the geographical feat as the beginning of the missionary enterprise.' The next step must be to plant inland, in healthy situations, permanent settlements of Europeans who would develop the country's resources and built up honest trade which would end forever the agonies of the yoked slaves.

Sekelutu had wanted all the 114 Makololo volunteers to go to England. Livingstone had regretfully to refuse, but he took the headman, Sekwetu. However, the waves, the storms and the tossing of the brig *Frolic* so alarmed this unhappy man that his mind gave way, and off Mauritius he threw himself overboard and was drowned. But in the brig, Livingstone felt 'at home in everything, except my own mother-tongue'. Three and a half years without speaking a word of English, except during his stay with Mr Gabriel, had made him so rusty that 'the words I wanted would not come to my call'. The *Frolic* left Quilemane on 12 July 1856, and took him to Mauritius where he stayed to recuperate from his enlarged spleen. In Cairo, he learned of the death of his father. He reached England on 9 December 1856, after an absence of almost exactly sixteen years, to find himself, to his astonishment and perplexity, a national hero.

Honours came thick and fast. Before he had been in England a week he received a Gold Medal from the Royal Geographical Society and a eulogy from its President, Sir Roderick Murchison, extolling not only his discoveries but his honourable conduct in refusing to abandon the Makololo in Luanda, thereby showing the world what stuff an English Christian was made of. The London Missionary Society honoured him the following day, with the famous philanthropist Lord Shaftesbury in the chair. Soon after came the Freedom of the City of

London and later, when his book was written, other Freedoms, honorary degrees, presentations and two Fellowships he valued highly: that of the Royal Faculty of Physicians and Surgeons in Glasgow, and to him, the highest award of all – Fellowship of the Royal Society.

After centuries of neglect by the British public, Africa had, almost suddenly it seemed, become fashionable. People no longer yawned when the topic was raised, or laughed as they had at James Bruce's stories about his discovery of the sources of the Blue Nile half a century earlier. Instead they reached for encyclopaedias, studied half-completed maps, raised funds for missionary societies and, when Livingstone brought out *Missionary Researches and Travels in South Africa* late in 1857, bought thirteen thousand copies in advance, at a guinea each, obliging John Murray to reprint seven times in quick succession.

The reason for this change was simple. At long last the so-called Dark Continent was yielding up secrets held inviolate since the days of the Pharoahs. And these were turning out to be less concerned with legends like King Solomon's mines and Prester John, with heathen rites, cannibals and queer goings-on generally, than with resources that could be developed for the profit of mankind, as well as for the profits of individual men. Scientists were excited about new plants, animals and rocks; geographers about new mountains, rivers and lakes; men of commerce about new customers ready to buy British goods and new sources of raw materials ready to be tapped; and philanthropists about the slave-trade, the one great blot on this scene of promise. There was something for everyone.

The European exploration of central Africa was entering upon its twenty years of greatest achievement. The origins of the Congo, of the Zambesi and, above all, of the Nile, were still a mystery and a challenge. It was the riddle of the Nile sources that had caught hold of the public imagination. Since the days of Herodotus, indeed before, people had been speculating about it. In 1857, Livingstone's first homecoming year, Burton and Speke left Zanzibar on the expedition which took them both to Lake Tanganyika, and Speke to his first glimpse of Lake Victoria; in 1862 Speke was to confirm his guess that this enormous lake gave birth to the White Nile. Baker was to look down on Lake Albert, another source, in 1864; Stanley to paddle down the Congo and emerge at its mouth in 1877.

In seven years of solitary and painful exploration, Livingstone did more than any other individual, before or since, to fill in the map of south central Africa, previously almost a blank from Kuruman to Timbuktu. This map, published in 1857, indicates his major journeys.

The time was therefore ripe to receive with intense interest and admiration this gaunt, awkward, indomitable Scot of humble birth who had gone alone into the 'heart of darkness', unsupported by any government or powerful body and animated by no thought of personal gain. In this he was unique, as in so many other ways. The great African explorers were a mixed bag with the usual mixed motives, but desire for fame and glory was a common denominator. Except for Livingstone. Moreover, at a period in history when almost everyone accepted Christianity, even if few put it into practice, here was a man who behaved like the best kind of Christian there could possibly be. In an age of materialism, here was a man who turned his back upon the Golden Calf to share his crust with the beggar and his cloak with the poor. A Christian gentleman, an English (albeit Scots) patriot, a healer of the sick, brave as a lion, modest, selfless as a saint: he seemed to combine in one person the virtues everyone revered. Here was the Happy Warrior 'that every man in arms should wish to be'. If Britain

93

could produce, and from its working class at that, a man of this calibre, Britain must indeed be the great, sound, honourable Christian nation of its citizens' wish. He stifled doubts: God was in his heaven, all was right with the British Isles, if not with the rest of the world.

The object of this adulation had intended to get back as soon as possible to the Zambesi to repatriate his waiting Makololo, but was persuaded that his duty lay first in writing a book. So after a burst of 'public spouting', and a visit to his family in Hamilton, he took lodgings in Sloane Street and settled down to a labour he found even more onerous than riding Sinbad through the Congo forests. It was done at great speed and consisted largely of edited slabs of his journal, but its vivid, robust and plain straightforward style – save when agonies of mind tempted him into the second person singular – make it enthralling reading to this day.

Now at last he was reunited with his own family. Almost every letter he had written to Mary, or she to him, had miscarried, and he cannot have known how desperate her plight had been during his four and a half years' absence. Perhaps he never did know; she was not one to complain. It is certain that she was dreadfully poor, at one time very seriously ill, almost friendless, and that she fell out, at an early stage, with the Livingstones in Hamilton and had no help from them. About a year after her arrival in England, Neil Livingston wrote to Tidman at the London Missionary Society to inquire after his grandchildren, 'having no other way of getting any word about them, as their mother was pleased to forbid all communication with us no less than three different times. . . . Owing to her remarkably strange conduct ever since we became acquainted with her, we have resolved to have no more intercourse with her until there is evidence that she is a changed person.' Nothing survives of Mary's side of the quarrel. Since her marriage, she had lived an independent, self-reliant life with her husband in the wilds, undisputed mistress of her little world; her four children, one born literally in an ox-wagon, were accustomed to the freedom, interest and sunshine of bush and desert; to re-make her life in the cold, grey outskirts of Glasgow on a bare pittance and under the censorious eye of elderly in-laws and two spinster sisters-in-law must have been almost impossible. So, indeed, she evidently found it, and existed with her family in cheap lodgings in Manchester, Kendal, Epsom and elsewhere, always on the edge of poverty or beyond it, friendless, forlorn, not knowing whether or no she was a widow and might have to continue for the rest of her life in this miserable state. No wonder her health gave way. Such a background makes all the more pathetic the verses she wrote to greet her husband on his return:

A hundred thousand welcomes, and it's time for you to come
From the far land of the foreigner, to your country and your
    home.
Oh, long as we were parted, ever since you went away,
I never passed an easy night, or knew an easy day.

Do you think I would reproach you with the sorrows that I bore?
Since the sorrow is all over now I have you here once more,
And there's nothing but the gladness and the love within my
    heart,
And hope so sweet and certain that never again we'll part.

A hundred thousand welcomes! How my heart is gushing o'er
With the love and joy and wonder just to see your face once
    more.
How did I live without you all those long long years of woe?
It seems as if t'would kill me to be parted from you now.

You'll never part me, darling, there's a promise in your eye;
I may tend you while I'm living, you will watch me when I die.
And if death but kindly lead me to the blessed home on high,
What a hundred thousand welcomes will await you in the sky!

'A hundred thousand welcomes'

In their Chelsea lodgings, the Livingstones spent the last months of domestic life as a family that they were to enjoy. And enjoy it they did. In the woods at Barnet the prodigal father romped with his children, suddenly disappearing into a 'ferny thicket' and coming out at some unexpected corner. 'The Doctor was sportive and fond of a joke, and Mrs Livingstone entered into his humour', recorded a friend with whom they stayed in Highbury. In society, they were both reserved and quiet: 'It was a great trial to Dr Livingstone to go to a grand dinner. He had not the appearance of a very strong man.' To grand dinners, however, he had to go, and make speeches, which he knew he did badly – his throat still troubled him. And he was mobbed in public places, just like a modern footballer or pop singer: even in church; on one occasion, though he kept his head down and covered his face with his hands, the preacher recognised him and foolishly said so, and after the service people scrambled over the pews to shake his hand.

When his book became a best-seller, he suddenly found himself rich. After setting aside a sum to support his widowed mother and help towards his children's education, he started to give the rest away. To his young brother-in-law John Moffat he gave £500, his wagon and £150 a year for the donor's life if Moffat would go at once as missionary to the Makololo. The offer was accepted, but it was to the Matebele and not the Makololo that the young man was sent. Livingstone never kept a lecture fee. When the Blantyre cotton workers invited him to address their Literary and Scientific Institute and paid him thirty guineas, he offered the money to equip 'a coffee-room on the plan of French cafés, where men, women and children may go, instead of to whisky shops. . . . . The sort I contemplate would suit poor young fellows who cannot have a comfortable fire at home.'

Most of his ideas were practical and shrewd. Hearing of his sister Janet's proposal to set up as a milliner, he had advised her from the wilds of Barotseland: 'One fashion or shape will not last long, however much you may excel at it', and urged her to go to Glasgow at least once a year to keep her eye in 'at the time the fashions change'. When members of the Manchester Chamber of Commerce cross-questioned him about commercial prospects in central Africa, he enumerated twenty-five new kinds of fruit he had brought back, and described to them oils, fibres, dyes and other products they had never heard of. They passed a unanimous resolution calling on the Government to give him 'facilities for further explorations in the interior of Africa', and soon a movement was under way to send the explorer back with official and financial support.

While waiting at Quilemane for a passage home, he had received a letter from his Directors which had given him a severe jolt. Sweetening the pill with praise, they had pointed out that the Society could not continue indefinitely to finance 'plans connected only remotely with the spread of the Gospel'. Livingstone's own reports had dwelt on the many serious obstacles to missionary effort in these unhealthy and remote places, and anyway the money was not there. The Society had overspent by £13,000 the year before, and Africa was only one, and by no means the most important, of its many fields. Almost as soon as he landed, he returned a dignified but pained reply, and wrote later to a friend: 'I will follow out the work in spite of

the veto of the Board. If it is according to the Will of God, means will be provided from other quarters.'

They were. Livingstone now had powerful friends, notably Sir Roderick Murchison, who took him to see the Foreign Secretary, the Earl of Clarendon. This was followed by a memorandum from Livingstone outlining a plan 'to make the Zambesi a path for commerce in the Interior and thus end the slave trade'. He drew up a shopping-list of things to take out 'to make a small beginning'; it included two or three cotton gins, several strong, malleable ploughs, two presses for extracting oil from groundnuts and two small pairs of rollers for extracting juice from sugar cane. The ultimate outcome was his appointment a year later (1858), at a salary of £500 a year, as HM Consul in Quilemane, and 'commander of an expedition for exploring Eastern and Central Africa, for the promotion of Commerce and Civilisation with a view to the extinction of the slave-trade'. Meanwhile, with mutual regrets, he had resigned from the London Missionary Society.

'Just come here and tell me what you want, and I will give it to you', the Foreign Secretary said at a reception; and he was as good as his word. In December 1857, Parliament voted £5,000, and orders were placed for a shallow-draught paddle-steamer and an iron house for stores, both to be taken out in sections. Appointments were settled for a staff of six besides the leader. These included Commander Norman Bedingfeld, as navigator; a twenty-year-old geologist, Richard Thornton, from the School of Mines; a brilliant young Scots doctor and botanist, John Kirk; the older Thomas Baines, already known for his Australian paintings, as artist and store-keeper; a Scots ships' engineer, George Rae. Finally, as 'moral agent' and general assistant, there was the leader's brother Charles, who was described as having 'had experience of cotton' in the United States – though hardly, one would think, in the parish of which he was pastor at Lakeville, New York. His age was thirty-six; he had graduated in Divinity at Oberlin College, Ohio, was married, with a family, and gave up a salary of £750 a year for one of £350 to join his brother's team.

The paddle-steamer was designed and built, at a cost of only £1,200, by Macgregor Laird of Birkenhead within five weeks. She was seventy-five feet long, eight feet in beam and with a draught of only two feet, capable of carrying thirty-six men and twelve tons of freight and powered by a twelve h.p. wood-

With the help of Murchison
(top left) Livingstone was
able to bring together the
talented work-force he
needed for the Expedition;
Thornton and Kirk (left);
Rae, Baines and
Tidman (right).

burning engine. She was called the *Ma-Robert*, the Bechuana name for Mary Livingstone. The personnel was mustered and everything assembled – the launch and iron house in sections, the stores, medicines, instruments and tools, bales of cloth, cotton seed to be distributed to chiefs, all the host of things needed for a two years' expedition – within three months.

One last point had meanwhile been dealt with. A Portuguese presence had been maintained in the Zambesi valley for over three hundred years. By this time it had worn very thin. Tete, established in the 1530s, had dwindled to less than thirty crumbling European houses, and Sena was even more down-at-heel. Nevertheless, the Portuguese claim to sovereignty over the lower Zambesi basin had never been disputed by a European Power. On the contrary, Britain had agreed only ten years earlier 'not to call in question the claims of Portugal to any territories on the eastern coast of Africa', provided Portugal allowed British warships to operate their anti-slavery patrols in Mozambique coastal waters.

Now an official British expedition was about to make its way up a river and into a hinterland where Portuguese sovereignty prevailed. Naturally, the Government in Lisbon had to be, at the very least, informed. It was remarkable that Clarendon, who seems to have fallen under Livingstone's spell, entrusted to the forthright missionary the task of drawing up a diplomatic memorandum. The missionary had made his views quite clear. 'In Eastern Africa,' he wrote to Clarendon, 'no vestige of their ancient authority remains.' He was also optimistic, to say the least, about the likely Portuguese reaction. They would welcome the opportunity, he thought, to develop 'resources of a fertile country from which they derive no benefit. Both countries, Britain and Portugal, could then go forward together.' The ancient allies should jointly set up new stations on the upper Zambesi and 'the river ought to be declared a free pathway for all nations'.

The fly in the ointment was the slave-trade. Portugal had not lagged behind other European nations in signing treaties and issuing proclamations and *portarias* to suppress it; they had dismissed many officials for failure to enforce these undertakings; but the trade obstinately continued, and some Portuguese officials undoubtedly took part. The only remedy, to pay its agents in Africa well enough to enable them to live decently without trading, was perhaps beyond the nation's resources; at

OPPOSITE While he was at Tete the artist Baines suffered acutely from malaria which often made him delirious and was accused by Livingstone, on very slender evidence, of misappropriating stores; but he was an industrious as well as a skilful painter, and recorded many scenes of African life.

Livingstone's return to England – 1856

Livingstone's happiest moments in England were those spent with his family whom he had not seen for five years. The publication of his *Missionary Researches, and Travels in South Africa*, and the interest aroused by his lectures, led to a public demand for his return to Africa with official backing.

RIGHT Pencil drawing of David Livingstone by J. Bonomi, 1857.

Freedom of City

TO THE

REVEREND DAVID LIVINGSTONE, M.D.

CITY HALL, 16th September, 1857,

AT ONE O'CLOCK.

ENTRY BY ALBION STREET.

JOHN STRANG, CHAMBERLAIN.

ABOVE One of the many tributes to Livingstone was the freedom of the city of Glasgow.

LEFT Dr Livingstone with
Mr Wilbraham Taylor, a
resident of Barnet, taken
at the time Livingstone
took a house nearby at
Hadley Green.

BELOW Livingstone with his
wife and children, 1857.

To convey men and stores up the Zambesi a shallow-draught paddle-steamer was built in record time, for only £1,200, by the Scots philanthropist Macgregor Laird. The vessel, named *Ma-Robert* – Mary Livingstone's Bechuana name – was loaded in sections in the steamship *Pearl* to be reassembled on the Zambesi.

any rate, it was not applied. The British conscience, as the Portuguese well knew, when aroused on a humanitarian issue, could be a formidable and often alarming phenomenon. Livingstone was plainly about to arouse it. The last thing they wanted was an expedition under his command poking about their colony and exposing all sorts of weak spots and dubious practices. On the other hand, the last thing they could afford was openly to obstruct a project with such worthy humanitarian and scientific aims. At this stage, Livingstone evidently had not realised how deeply implicated in the trade many of the Portuguese in Africa had become; when realisation dawned, he was all the more outraged. A series of polite interchanges ended in a Portuguese promise of free passage for the expedition as far as Tete, and of general support, but restricted the leader's consular powers to Quilemane, excluding Tete and Sena. Portuguese rights were re-affirmed to the territory, re-named

Zambesia, lying between the coast and the ruins of Zumbo, rather more than two hundred miles above Tete.

Before the expedition got away, Livingstone delivered the most famous of his lectures to a packed audience in the Senate House at Cambridge on 4 December 1857. It was not so much a lecture as a jerkily delivered series of observations on the peoples, languages and geography of central Africa, 'expressive of thoughts which he could not arrange in set periods'. But when he reached his peroration, he shouted out the final sentence and abruptly sat down. After a few moments of stunned silence, there was 'a great explosion of cheering never surpassed in this building'. Livingstone had declared: 'I beg to direct your attention to Africa. I know that in a few years I shall be cut off in that country, which is now open. Do not let it be shut again! I go back to Africa to try to make a path for commerce and Christianity. Do you carry on the work which I have begun. I leave it with you!' From this lecture was born the Universities Mission to Central Africa, jointly formed by the Universities of Cambridge, Oxford, Dublin and Durham.

Finally, to set the seal of national approval, there was an audience with the Queen. Livingstone attended 'without ceremony, in his black coat and blue trousers', but he had exchanged the 'plain midshipman's cap' which for the last sixteen years had covered his head when on his travels, for a consul's cap, much the same but with a band of gold lace round it. (He never wore the 'new-fangled coal-scuttle helmet', or topee, that was coming in from India about this time.) For half an hour the Queen 'conversed affably' with the explorer and was amused; she 'laughed heartily' when he told her that the Bechuana, informed that Livingstone's own chief was very rich, asked how many cows she had.

And so with royal approval, official backing and high hopes, the steamship *Pearl* left Liverpool on 12 March 1858, on an expedition that was to last six years instead of the intended two; to embrace triumph and disaster, but more of disaster; to confound many cherished hopes; and eventually to add to the British Empire a large slice of fertile, and as yet unknown, Africa.

5 Back to the Zambesi

A FEW DAYS OUT OF LIVERPOOL, the expedition's leader read
the Foreign Office's general instructions, which he had
drafted himself, to his team, and added specific ones of his own
to each member. 'The main object of the Expedition is to extend
the knowledge already attained of the geography and mineral
and agricultural resources of Eastern and Central Africa.' They
were also to make contacts with chiefs, to establish the best
possible relations with the native peoples and to set them an
example in orderly Christian living. A plan of operations,
approved by Lord Clarendon, read:

The Expedition is to pass rapidly through the unhealthy area of
the Lower Zambesi, deposit its heavy baggage at Tete, visit the
leading chiefs above Tete, and proceed to the Kebrabasa Rapids to
discover whether the launch would be able to steam up there when
the river is high. The iron house is then to be erected on a suitable
site above the confluence of the Zambesi and the Kafue to serve as a
central depot. Further exploration is then to be undertaken towards
the source of the Zambesi and up the rivers flowing into it from the
north, in order to ascertain whether the network of waters reported
by the natives exists or not.

Agricultural experiments and religious instruction were also to
be conducted at the central depot, and the members would
have the option of returning to England when their two years
were up.

In a private letter to Professor Sedgwick of Cambridge,
Livingstone admitted that his aims 'have something more in
them than meets the eye. They are not merely exploratory, for
I go with the intention of benefiting both the African and my
own countrymen.' His ultimate object was to plant 'an English
colony in the healthy highlands of Central Africa. (I have told
it only to the Duke of Argyle.)' He had told it also to his journal;
it was his dearest aim. Only thus could civilisation and Christianity take root; only thus could the slave-trade be killed, not
merely scotched.

Livingstone could not forbear to lecture his assistants – 'we
come among them [Africans] as members of a superior race and
servants of a Government that desires to elevate the more
degraded portions of the human family' – but added bits of
down-to-earth advice. Chiefs should always be respected, and
presents of food accepted: 'it is impolitic to allow the ancient
custom of feeding strangers to go into disuse'. Kirk, the doctor,

was to keep on good terms with witch-doctors, 'generally the most observant people to be met with', never to disparage their treatment in front of a patient and generally to treat them as colleagues rather than quacks – Livingstone's invariable practice. One of his injunctions was much in advance of its time: 'I would earnestly impress on every member of the Expedition a sacred regard to life, and never to destroy it unless some good end is to be answered by its extinction; the wanton waste of animal life I have witnessed . . . makes me anxious that this Expedition should not be guilty of similar abominations.'

Nothing in the leader's experience had prepared him for a task of this kind, and little in his character, it might be thought, suited him to it. A lone wolf, he was now put in charge of a pack. At forty-five, he had never had Europeans under his command before, and in his life as a missionary had, wherever possible, avoided them in his determination to go 'beyond another man's lines'. Africans, it was true, trusted, respected and followed him to a remarkable degree. But Africans, or at any rate those he had dealt with, followed, respected and obeyed their chief. Any inclination not to do so had long ago been stamped out. Livingstone had always been a surrogate chief, either through force of character or because, as in the cases of Sebituane and Sekelutu, he was their friend and so invested with their authority. Europeans had a wholly different approach. They respected him both as a man and as a leader; they were under his orders; but they would speak their mind.

Nor had Livingstone any administrative experience. Delegation, like team-work, was something he can have known little about. He was accustomed, under God, to absolute self-reliance, believing that if he did his duty to the utmost, God would see that 'all will come right in the end'. He was not dictatorial, but the reverse; he felt that people of intelligence knew best how to do their job in their own way. His standards were very high, and his modesty prompted the belief that if he could do a thing, or put up with a discomfort, or overcome an obstacle, others could do so just as well. This was far from being the case.

Mary and the six-year-old Oswell sailed with him from Liverpool. The first disappointment was that Mary was desperately seasick, and found to be pregnant again. Her husband was taken aback: 'This is a great trial to me. Had she come with us, she might have proved of essential service to the

David Livingstone, from a
contemporary photograph.

Until she disintegrated at the end of 1860, the
paddle-steamer *Ma-Robert* was the Expedition's floating
and uncomfortable home. Despite a draught of only two
feet, she was frequently aground on mud banks,
as Baines recorded in a sketch made on 24 May 1858.

expedition in cases of sickness and otherwise, but it may all turn out for the best.' Apparently merely aggrieved at the loss of an unpaid nurse, more probably his true feelings were revealed when he wrote, after leaving her at the Cape, 'it was a bitter parting with my wife, like tearing the heart out of one'. The Moffats were in Cape Town, where the Governor gave him a grand dinner and he was presented with a silver box containing eight hundred guineas raised by public subscription – a contrast indeed with the hostility and suspicion he had met with from colonial officials six years before. He handed Mary over to her parents, who took her to Kuruman where, in the following November, she gave birth to a daughter, Anna Mary. It was arranged, in so far as such arrangements could be made, that husband and wife would meet at Linyanti in about a year's time, when Livingstone would go up the river to restore the Makololo to their chief, and fetch Mary down to join him in the *Ma-Robert*.

The mouth of the Zambesi is a delta with four main channels, and the expedition's first discovery was that even the deepest of these, the Kongone, was too shallow and blocked with mangroves to be navigated by a vessel of ordinary draught such as the *Pearl*. So Livingstone's basic premise, that the river would become 'God's highway' for the passage of Christianity and commerce into the far interior, was put in question at the start. Far from being able to convey the heavy stores three hundred miles inland to Tete, the *Pearl* could get no further than an island in a mosquito-ridden swamp forty miles from the bar. There was nothing for it but to unload the sections of the *Ma-Robert*, put them together and establish a depot at this spot – Expedition Island – instead of at Tete.

This was a serious setback, for it meant that all the stores would have to be taken up-river in instalments in the small, wood-burning and, as it turned out, ill-constructed launch, causing long delays in the hot, malarial coastal swamps. The health of the expedition was the leader's first concern. A daily dose of two grains of quinine in half a glass of sherry was prescribed for all members from the day they reached the river's mouth in May 1858. This might not (and did not) offer protection, but it would, the Doctor believed, make the fever, once contracted, easier to bring under control when treated with his famous mixture (made up into pills which became known as 'Zambesi rousers') followed by repeated doses of

ABOVE The Expedition's first port of call was Cape Town, the graceful colonial capital whose main street as it appeared in the early nineteenth century is depicted here. Livingstone left Mary and their small son Oswell at the Cape with the Moffats, while he continued in the *Pearl* to the mouth of the Zambesi.

OPPOSITE Pandanus or screw palm, covered with climbing plants, near the Kongone Canal of the Zambesi. Livingstone forced a passage through the Kongone, with great difficulty, being obliged to break a lifelong principle and work on Sundays.

quinine until symptoms of deafness and singing in the ears appeared. But he held that 'a much more important precaution than quinine is constant employment and sufficient bodily exercise to produce perspiration every day'.

It was vital to get the expedition as quickly as possible through the mangrove swamps. To this he sacrificed one of his most cherished principles, and everyone worked throughout a Sunday. 'People, I hear, blame me for this', he wrote later, 'but they would have blamed me much more if I had lost nearly all the Expedition.' It was gruelling work in the scorching sun and steamy atmosphere, but in his opinion good for everyone. The *Ma-Robert* was assembled, stores unloaded, the iron house erected on Expedition Island and the *Pearl* sailed away. Then the first load of stores was taken in the *Ma-Robert* to establish a base at Shupanga, about seventy miles upstream, clear of the delta but still some five hundred miles below the Zambesi's junction with the Kafue where they had hoped it would be.

Troubles soon assailed the Expedition almost as thickly as mosquitoes. Commander Bedingfeld was the first casualty. On closer acquaintance he proved to be a touchy, self-important character who, as an officer of the Royal Navy, did not happily accept a missionary's orders. Livingstone reacted sharply to the arrogance and irascibility of the former friend he now called 'an unmitigated muff, [who] thought we could not move a mile without him and assumed all manner of airs. I mounted the

paddle-box and sent him home to nurse his dignity there. . . .
I never met such a fool and a liar, and yet all in combination
with extra ostentatious piety.' Bedingfeld went home not to
nurse his dignity but to justify his conduct and blame his former
leader. After an inquiry, Livingstone was upheld, and
Bedingfeld's superior at the Admiralty wrote in a private letter
that he did not consider him any great loss to the Expedition.
He had been twice court-martialled for insubordination in his
career. On the other hand, Livingstone had hardly been tactful
when, during an acrimonious correspondence, he had offered
the Commander 'a hint. . . . With the change of climate there is
often a peculiar condition of the bowels which makes the
individual imagine all sorts of things in others. Now I earnestly
and most respectfully recommend you to try a little aperient
medicine occasionally and you will find it much more soothing
than writing official letters.' This advice, the angry Com-

The *Pearl* could get no further than a flat, unhealthy island near the mouth of the Kongone, named Expedition Island, where a base was established, the stores unloaded and the *Ma-Robert* put together. Livingstone had intended the base to be above Tete, near the confluence of the Kafue with the Zambesi.

mander retorted, 'had been better addressed to a child'. But he put his finger on a fundamental weakness in the Expedition's leadership when he wrote that 'most of the misunderstandings would have been avoided had you treated me as your second-in-command and allowed me to know your plans and see your wishes carried out'.

Bedingfeld's departure left the Expedition without a navigator, but Livingstone 'mounted the paddle-box' and took over. He would have been more at home, he said, driving a cab in a London fog in November, and was liable to call out 'starboard' when he meant 'port'. But he navigated the launch successfully for over sixteen hundred miles.

The next member of the Expedition to disappoint his hopes was the *Ma-Robert* herself. She devoured prodigious quantities of wood which took far too many laborious hours to cut; four hours were needed for her under-powered engines to get up steam, and she proceeded at a slower speed than a canoe. She chuffed and wheezed so much that she was quickly re-named the Asthmatic. Back and forth she had to go, taking up supplies at first to Shupanga, where the ever-helpful Major Secard had put a good house at their disposal, and later on to Tete. Fever soon incapacitated the Europeans, especially Baines, who became repeatedly delirious, and Charles Livingstone. Kirk and Rae accompanied Livingstone to Tete, which they reached on 8 September, to receive an ecstatic welcome from the surviving Makololo whose faith in their leader's return had never faltered. But thirty men had died of smallpox and six had been killed on the orders of a chief. Livingstone prayed for them and for himself: 'Grant, Lord, that I may be more faithful to them that remain. They have lots of pigs and say if they were only oxen we should be content.'

Before taking them back to Sekelutu's, the Kebrabasa rapids had to be investigated. Livingstone knew by now that they were a formidable obstacle but believed that they could be made navigable by blasting out the rocks. Early in November, accompanied by Kirk, Rae, a naval quartermaster who had joined the Expedition and some Makololo volunteers, he entered the gorge on foot. It was a fantastic, awe-inspiring place with great, contorted, polished-looking rocks towering eighty or a hundred feet above the river, which was broken into a whole series of cataracts. Two days were spent clambering over rocks so hot as to blister the skin, and they returned to Tete exhausted and bitterly disappointed. It was clear that no amount of blasting would overcome this impediment. 'God's highway' was closed.

Morale at Tete was beginning to flag. Everyone had incessant fever and tempers were frayed. The leader himself developed an irritating skin disease and fell into one of his moods of despair which he concealed from his colleagues but confided to his journal: 'The Kebrabasa is what I never expected. No hint of its nature ever reached my ears. . . . What we shall do if this is to be the end of the navigation I cannot now divine, but here I am, and I am trusting in Him who never made ashamed those who did so.' What he did was to go back and look at the rapids again. Though the gorge might be impassable while the river

Livingstone's hopes of navigating the river as far as the Victoria Falls were shattered when, for the first time, he saw the savage Kebrabasa rapids above Tete. He was forced to turn his attention to the river's main tributary.

was low, when floods came down in the wet season it might yet be navigable. In fact, it *had* to be navigable; his whole plan depended on it; God's highway could not be closed.

So back he went with Kirk, four Makololo and some reluctant guides. The rocks were perpendicular, scorching hot and rent by dangerous crevices. The first day they climbed fifteen hundred feet and descended a thousand feet before breakfasting off a biscuit and a little chocolate, at which point the guides and three of the Makololo fell out. Livingstone, Kirk and one of the men scrambled on and took three hours to go a mile. The rocks were literally too hot to touch and Kirk persuaded his leader, who was like a man possessed, to return to camp and make a fresh attempt in the morning. They slept beside the river which,

they calculated, would rise eighty feet when in flood. Next day
they struggled on, taking the whole morning to reach the next
bend. 'Dr L. never knew such work in his life', Kirk recorded.
'We passed among and over and under these slippery hot rocks,
then ascending what was practically a precipice, chiefly by the
roots of bushes, for 200 feet. If one man had fallen, all under
must have gone to the bottom.' Beyond the bend lay yet another
cataract confined between steep, inaccessible walls. There was
nothing for it but to return, defeated, to the launch. Even now,

The *Ma-Robert* on the Zambesi
above Senna, with the
saddle-shaped hill
Kevramisa in the distance.

Livingstone did not give in. Somehow or other, these rapids
must be overcome: if not at low water, then in flood; if not by a
feeble little launch like the *Ma-Robert*, then by a bigger one
with a speed of twelve or fourteen knots. In a dispatch to the
Foreign Office, he gave his opinion that a suitable vessel
would pass up the rapids 'without difficulty in January or
February', and asked the Foreign Secretary to supply one.
If the Government refused, then he would get a vessel
built and pay for it himself. He wrote to his old friend James

Murchison Falls

It was remarked that Livingstone formed with Sir Roderick Murchison a relationship resembling that of a highlander towards the chief of his clan. He named the cataract discovered by the Expedition on the Shiré river after his distinguished friend.

Young authorising him to spend up to £2,000 on the project.

Since nothing more could be done until a new vessel arrived, Livingstone decided to explore the Zambesi's tributaries in the hope that one of these might offer an alternative way to the interior. The obvious choice was the Shiré, which joined the Zambesi between Sena and Shupanga and whose waters were 'clean and black' instead of muddy – indicating, surely, some highland birth-place. An added attraction was that it had never been explored by the Portuguese. So, on New Year's Day 1859, Livingstone and Kirk entered the Shiré river in the launch on the start of an exploration that was to lead to momentous discoveries darkened by tragedy. After little more than a week's progress they found their way again blocked by rapids, which they called after Sir Roderick Murchison, and were informed by a friendly chief, Chibisa, of two lakes that lay beyond, which no white man had visited. So they returned to Tete to bring up reinforcements and make an assault on the lakes.

122

By now the launch was leaking as well as wheezing and had been pronounced unriverworthy by the engineer, Rae. Thornton, Baines and Charles Livingstone had been prostrated off and on by fever and had to remain at Tete, with Charles in charge. Accompanied by Kirk, two petty officers lent from HMS *Lynx* and fourteen Makololo, Livingstone got the *Ma-Robert* down the river and up the Shiré to the Murchison cataracts, where they moored her near Chibisa's village. From there, Kirk and Livingstone marched north-east for a fortnight and were rewarded by the sight of a beautiful lake cupped by mountains. This was Lake Shirwa. 'Lake Ngami is a mere pond to it', Livingstone noted; but Shirwa was a mere pond to another lake beyond, known to the Manganja as 'the lake of stars'. Leaving its discovery for a third sortie, they rejoined the *Ma-Robert* and took her down to the Kongone in the hope of finding mail and stores, but there was nothing, so, with frequent stops for wooding, they wheezed and puffed up again to Tete.

They found their colleagues in a sorry state. All through the unhealthy rainy season, January to April, they had been victims of fever. Baines had been frequently delirious and Thornton had succumbed to several attacks of hysteria 'resembling exactly that met with in females'. Charles had proved an incompetent, selfish leader and everyone had quarrelled. Fresh food had often been short, downpours continual, and

ABOVE The Shiré valley was populated by the Manganja tribe, whose women distorted their upper lips by inserting rings.

BELOW After her assembly at the mouth of the Kongone the *Ma-Robert* was taken up the river as far as Tete.

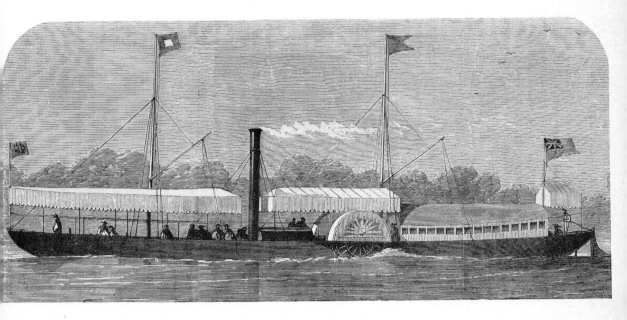

both doctors had been away. The only thing on which they seemed to agree was in disliking Charles Livingstone. Even Kirk, the most level-headed of the team, found him 'horribly disagreeable company'. He seems to have been incorrigibly idle, to have shirked such duties as he had and to have been arrogant and overbearing. But what exactly were his duties? Thornton as geologist was busy collecting specimens, and discovered and opened a seam of coal. Baines was a conscientious artist and had the stores to see to. But what a 'moral agent' was supposed to do was unclear. His brother gave him odd jobs – looking for gold, and making a collection of birds. Although in Holy Orders, he seems to have made no attempt to save souls. There were plenty of Makololo probably in need of salvation.

If his hands indeed were idle, the devil found work in poisoning his brother's mind against Baines. Deficiencies in the stores had come to light, and Baines was accused of having misappropriated them and sold them to Portuguese. Baines denied the charge indignantly and the main evidence seems to have been a 'confession' that Charles (and Charles alone) claimed to have heard while Baines was delirious. But David sided against Baines and threatened dismissal if Baines should 'again go off skylarking with the Portuguese' or spend the expedition's time and money painting Portuguese portraits. The dispute dragged on, concerning itself with such matters as a missing length of canvas and five cases of loaf-sugar, until November 1859, when Baines was sent home. For the next seven years he continued to protest his innocence. Meanwhile, Richard Thornton had also been dismissed. On his return from the Shiré, Livingstone noted in his journal: 'Thornton doing nothing: is inveterately lazy and wants good sense.' (Thornton's legs had been covered with sores, and he had continued to work the coal.) So in June he left, to refute the charges by tramping to Zanzibar and then taking part with credit in an exploration of Mt Kilimanjaro. At his own request, he rejoined the Expedition eighteen months later, and died of fever at Chibisa's in April 1863, at the age of twenty-six.

For these and other troubles the leader was inevitably blamed. The contrast between his tact and patience with Africans and his sometimes dour and unsympathetic treatment of fellow-whites has often been remarked upon. In part his shyness was to blame, his deep reserve. Europeans demanded so much more than African tribesmen. He had no wish, far

While Livingstone, Kirk and Rae explored the upper Shiré, Charles, Baines and Thornton remained at Tete. Here Richard Thornton, the geologist, opened a seam of coal, and Baines painted the scene.

from it, to offend anyone's susceptibilities. But he lacked the light touch, the art of administering a rebuke gracefully and the spirit of cameraderie. Duty was duty, and always the stern daughter of the voice of God. At a later stage of the Expedition, Charles attacked his brother for failing to give a lead to the others, who were 'always at a loss how to act'. David replied that he believed in letting people 'do their duty in their own way; it is irksome to most men to be driven as soldiers and sailors are'. And despite the unbending strength of that will of steel, he was not immune from the depressing, and sometimes unbalancing, effects of chronic and prolonged sickness. 'Very ill with bleeding from the bowels and purging', runs an entry in his journal during the period of his dispute with Baines. 'Bled all night. Got up at one a.m. to take latitude.' Hardly a recipe for tolerance and an even temper. 'Bad health and a touch of fever is nothing,' wrote Kirk, 'were it not for the bad humour it puts everyone in, and sickness is a thing with which the Doctor has no patience, either in himself or anyone else . . . if his digestive system don't go alright, he loses his diplomatic power wonderfully' – as the Doctor himself had pointed out to Bedingfeld.

ABOVE The Commandant at Tete put a house at the Expedition's disposal, in which its members lived when in this Portuguese settlement. They suffered from severe fevers, and in the case of Charles Livingstone from having too little to do.

But David Livingstone was never idle, and during his sojourn at Tete, learnt the dialect of the local people and compiled the first vocabulary (right).

Morumbuana = a boy <u>Tette</u> language

Mosikana – a girl

NaMoari – virgin

Oava = hear

Machuvbele = old women

Puia   a slave = a master

Okshena – white = Osuipa black.

shuvolomo –

Shimote – tree grand

Kamute = little tree

a mute – a tree

Agono   little.

Zaia kono come here
dina buera pomo – I will come here

Juma – forehead

Goto – hindhead

Maputu cheeks

Kope = face

dinaza I will come = vira

Dinaza kari – I came longago

Sidaenda zulu I went yesterd

Dine enda lero – I go today

In mid-July 1859, Livingstone with his brother, Kirk and Rae plus two seamen and some Makololo, left Tete in the now disintegrating launch, which they patched up as best they could by tying canvas bags stuffed with clay over the many holes in her hull. More insatiable than ever in her appetite for wood, she crawled back up the Shiré to Chibisa's (now Chikwawa), leaking from below and so drenched from above that the party sheltered under umbrellas in the cabin, and many of Kirk's botanical specimens were ruined by wet or eaten by cockroaches which also nibbled the men's legs at night and caused sores. Livingstone sought consolation in reading *Punch*. The two brothers and Kirk were thankful to leave the launch at Chibisa's with Rae in charge, and start overland for the 'lake of stars'.

They marched across part of the Shiré highlands and were delighted by their beauty, fertility and potential wealth. The people smelted iron and there were forges and furnaces everywhere. There was also cotton, and could be corn, indigo, oilseeds and sugar cane. Moreover it was cool and healthy, rising to seven thousand feet on Mt Zomba. Here at last was the region that had been sought so long and so diligently, the ideal site for European settlements. Livingstone's spirits revived. 'I have a very strong desire', he wrote in his journal 'to commence a system of colonisation of the honest poor; I would give £2,000 or £3,000 for the purpose. Intend to write to my friend Young about it. . . . It is a monstrous evil that all our healthy, handy, blooming daughters of England have not a fair chance, at least, to become the centres of domestic affections' – yet the 'ugliest huzzies in creation' were sent from workhouses to populate new worlds. 'My heart yearns over our own poor when I see so much of God's fair earth unoccupied', he wrote to Maclear. They marched for three weeks through country whose inhabitants were suspicious and at times threatening, and on 17 September 1859, set eyes on Lake Nyasa (now Malawi) – probably the Expedition's major geographical find.

They also discovered something of greater importance to the leader: a hitherto unsuspected focus of the slave-trade. On their way to the lake, they encountered gangs of captives whose necks were fastened into forked sticks, the other end of each stick being held by the slave immediately behind. The slavers were Arabs or Swahilis based on Zanzibar. One of the villagers offered to sell a man to the explorers for a fathom (six

'My heart yearns over our own poor when I see so much of God's fair earth unoccupied.'

yards) of red cloth. They came also upon the slavers' spoor: burnt villages, rotting corpses and vulture-picked skeletons. The southern end of Lake Nyasa was a meeting-place for several slave routes. Livingstone immediately conceived a plan to stop the trade by putting an armed launch on the lake itself and arranging to buy up all available supplies of ivory: for it was 'only by the ivory being carried by the slaves that the latter do not eat up all the profits of a trip'. It was an imaginative plan and its author wasted no time in urging it upon others, but wrote at once to the invaluable Young to ask him to get a suitable vessel built and commissioned at a cost of up to £6,000 of his own money. He wrote to Moffat:

I am working towards an object which some can see at a glance, others turn up the whites of their eyes at it. But my God may in mercy permit me to benefit both Africa and England on a scale that at first sight may appear impossible. Some poor noodles place it all to the love of exploration and seeking the glory that cometh from man. Let it stand over to be judged on that day when the secrets of all hearts shall be revealed.

When he got back to Chibisa's, he was a sick man, displaying symptoms of the disorder, bleeding from the bowels, that would ultimately kill him. After foot-slogging for 250 miles on very poor food, the others were exhausted too. But they took the decrepit launch down to the delta where they found a warship with mail and stores. She took off the unfortunate Baines who had been brought down from Tete. Shortly afterwards, Rae went home to supervise the building of the new vessel, to be called the *Lady Nyassa* and launched upon the lake of her name. Rae had 'behaved exceedingly well all the time he has been with us', and even offered to invest his savings in the new vessel; on the way home he was shipwrecked and lost all he possessed. The *Ma-Robert*, eating up more wood than ever, wheezed her way with difficulty back to Tete, her company reduced to eating salt beef and rotten pork because the slave raiders had so denuded the riverine population that nothing could be bought 'for love or money, in a country the fertility of which is astonishing'.

The time had come for Livingstone to redeem his promise to the Makololo. Kirk observed that the Doctor 'seems little inclined for this tramp'. Kirk himself was glum, but although his two years were up and he was free to go, he 'should not think of leaving the Doctor alone at this time'. He foresaw 'little but fatigue and hardship, perhaps sickness, and all for nothing tangible. . . . It is a clear case of "Kismet" and must be patched up as best I can into something useful.' The Makololo were no more enthusiastic. Most of them had taken local wives, bred children, made gardens and settled comfortably into their new surroundings. At Linyanti their former wives would certainly have remarried. About one-third either refused to leave Tete or decamped during the first few days. "All seemed disposed to go back', Livingstone noted on 25 May 1860, ten days after leaving Tete. 'They grumble perpetually, and make the journey excessively disagreeable.'

'They grumble perpetually and make the journey excessively unagreeable.'

It was not only the Makololo who disillusioned Livingstone. 'My brother keeping up his sulks', he wrote on 9 June. This was the first reference in the journal to Charles's abrasive behaviour. But now David admitted: 'I am at a loss how to treat him. As an assistant he has been of no value. Photography very unsatisfactory. Magnetism still more so. Meteorological observations not creditable, and writing the journal in arrears. In going up with us now he is useless, as he knows nothing of Portuguese or the native language.' His worst fault seems to have lain in backbiting and making trouble between his brother and other members of the team. Anyone else would have been sent packing long ago. Family loyalty had blinded the leader to his brother's faults to an extraordinary degree. Once away from the launch and all its worries, however, his spirits rose and the naturalist in him took over. Nothing was too great or too small for comment: the antics of a drunken ferryman, the structure of an ant's mandible. He was fascinated by ants, and found that they could communicate by chirruping as well as by movements of their antennae, in fact that they had a form of sound language. His life was still charmed. When marching without his gun, a rhino charged him, and unaccountably stopped dead within a few paces.

They passed again the ruins of Zumbo with their reminder of human failure and, much more depressing, of the failure of God's message to change the hearts of men. For the human condition was worse now, not better, than it had been when the Jesuits had abandoned their monastery for the ants and elements to crumble. Slavery had been added to the toll of man's inhumanities to man. It was about this time that he made the discovery, or perhaps faced the fact, that his own actions were spreading the slave-trade instead of destroying it. Until his

Livingstone's
Zambesi
Expedition
1858-64

coming, Portuguese subjects had not attempted to penetrate the upper Zambesi or the Shiré valleys, and so the trade in which they were, as Livingstone now realised, deeply involved, had not spread to those regions. But now that he had shown the way it was the slavers, not Christianity and beneficial commerce, who were following. Not far behind him, on this very journey, was a party of native Portuguese subjects pretending to be 'his children' and bartering ivory for slaves.

RIGHT Apart from slaves, ivory was the staple of the Arab and Swahili traders. Tusks like these could weigh 100 lb and more, and were being carried out in enormous quantities from central Africa by the slavers' caravans.

OPPOSITE Much of the slave trade was in the hands of 'black Arabs', Swahilis from Zanzibar and the East African coast who had adopted Arab dress and customs, but retained much of their native savagery.

'In opening the country through which no Portuguese durst previously pass, we were made the unwilling instruments of extending the slave-trade', he admitted. 'It was with bitter sorrow that we saw the good we would have done turned to evil.' By now his previous euphoric feelings about the Portuguese had been replaced by an implacable enmity – not towards individuals, who for the most part remained friendly and hospitable, but towards Portuguese misrule, corruption, immorality and above all connivance, at the very least, in the trade. He was, moreover, convinced that the Government in Lisbon, while promising to support the Expedition, had sent secret

instructions to Mozambique to do no such thing. The Expedition had become altogether too political for their liking, and its leader more and more outspoken in condemning all things Portuguese.

Within three months, the party was back at the Victoria Falls, admiring, re-measuring and unexpectedly encountering a solitary white man, under hut arrest by the local chief because he had swum in the river; the chief feared that crocodiles would eat the white man and he would get the blame when the English returned. The errant swimmer turned out to be a Mr Baldwin from Natal, who had walked there, guided by a compass, to see what Livingstone had discovered. Now here was the discoverer in person, who quickly had Mr Baldwin set free.

Here they heard that Sekelutu was ill. They found the chief covered in sores due probably to leprosy, but possibly to a severe form of eczema. The two white doctors treated him as best they could, and succeeded in cleaning up his sores. 'Yet the disease still remained', Kirk noted, 'and I believe will return now we are gone.' He was evidently right, for Sekelutu, still a young man, died four years later.

Even more distressing news had reached them meanwhile: of the destruction of the mission sent to the Makololo, as a result of Livingstone's enthusiasm, the year before. Robert Moffat had advised against sending a party of young missionaries without a doctor and without previous experience to such a distant and unhealthy spot. In the disregard of his advice, no doubt reliance on Livingstone's favourable reports about the Makololo, and about Sekelutu's helpfulness, had played a decisive part. Two young couples, one with four children and one with a baby, set out from Kuruman expecting to find Livingstone at Linyanti, although he had given no firm undertaking. At least Sekelutu, they felt sure, would welcome them. Sekelutu did no such thing. He robbed them of their food and clothing and even of their wagon, and kept them in the malarial swamps instead of conducting them to the healthy Batonga highlands where Livingstone had recommended that the mission should go. Inevitably, fever attacked them, and everyone died except one of the men and two now orphaned children, who managed to struggle back to Kuruman.

At Shesheke, Sekelutu told his friend a very different story: how he had liked and helped the leader, Mr Helmore, and

Thomas Baines visited the Victoria Falls in 1862, and painted this scene of a couple of unusually trim explorers in a dug-out canoe on the river above the Falls.

'wished to be acquainted with him – a very natural desire – before moving to the Highlands, and hence the delay which ended so fatally'. Livingstone simply could not believe that his friend the chief and his beloved Makololo could behave in such a dastardly way. Because Sekelutu again welcomed Livingstone so cordially, even offering to set aside a part of his country for Europeans, he thought the chief loved and welcomed all white men, and certainly all missionaries. But it was David Livingstone the chief loved, not the white men in general, and not the Helmores' party whom he had virtually killed.

The return journey from Linyanti to Kebrabasa was uneventful as African travel goes, except when Charles kicked one of the escort provided by Sekelutu and was very nearly speared. But at Kebrabasa the journey almost ended in that ill-omened cataract. Livingstone's men were by now experienced in the art of shooting rapids in canoes, and embarked confidently on the upper reaches rather than scramble with difficulty over the rocks. But things went wrong, there was a

Moose-oa-tunya (Victoria falls, Zam
taken from point D

A photograph of the Victoria
Falls taken in 1892 by W.F.Fry.

general mix-up and all the canoes overturned, hurling their occupants against the rocks to be sucked under the surging waters. Their escape was quite miraculous. No one drowned, but almost everything was swept away, including all Kirk's specimens and notes, virtually the whole botanical harvest of the Expedition. All he saved was a copy of Lindley's *Vegetable Kingdom*, a bag of pipe-lighters and a rifle. All their food went, and they became so famished that Kirk staved off a fainting fit only by sucking the discarded rind of a fruit someone else had eaten. At last, their clothes in rags, their boots worn through, they reached Tete, almost exactly six months after leaving it and after a march of fourteen hundred miles. 'We have kept faith with the Makololo', Kirk wrote to Murchison, 'though we have done nothing else.' The greater part of 1860, his leader feared, had been thrown away.

6 The Fight against Slavery

NEWS WHICH REKINDLED EVERYONE'S OPTIMISM was awaiting them at Tete, which they reached on 23 November 1860. A dispatch from Lord John Russell at the Foreign Office informed them that a vessel to replace the *Ma-Robert* was already on its way. The importance of the discoveries of Lake Nyasa and the Shiré highlands was recognised. Livingstone had suggested that the River Rovuma, north of the Zambesi, might lead into these highlands and so enable Portuguese territory to be altogether avoided; he was now authorised to investigate. Although his two years' commission had expired, the Expedition was to continue, and with increased support. Finally, best news of all, a letter from the Bishop of Cape Town informed him that the Universities Mission to Central Africa was sending out a party headed by a bishop to start work in the highlands he had so glowingly described. 'I am tired of discovery when no fruit follows', he had written. Here was the first fruit at last.

The whole party at Tete set out for the coast without delay in the *Ma-Robert*, now barely holding together. A few days before Christmas, she grounded on a sandbank and this time no amount of plugging and bailing could save her. She heeled over and sank. No one was sorry to see the last of her. They spent the next week in torrential rain getting the stores down to Senna in canoes lent by a helpful Portuguese. Three weeks later HMS *Sidon* arrived with the *Pioneer*, their new vessel, followed on 30 January 1861, by HMS *Lyra*, with the Bishop and four assistants. Charles Mackenzie, aged only thirty-six and the first missionary bishop to be consecrated, was an immediate success with everyone: tall, enthusiastic, energetic, gay, Kirk thought him 'a trump of a fellow' and Livingstone found him so congenial that 'they chaff each other all day like school-boys'.

But now there was another disappointment: the *Pioneer* was soundly built but her five-foot draught was too much for these shallow waters. They got only thirty miles up the Rovuma river and then had to turn back and proceed, after all, up the Zambesi and into the Shiré. Here the *Pioneer* continually grounded and had to be hauled off mudbank after mudbank, a single one of which took a fortnight to overcome. Six weeks were occupied with anchor and cable in coaxing the vessel the last fifty miles to Chibisa's village. 'We have been aground about as many hours as we have been afloat', wrote the Bishop,

PREVIOUS PAGES In 1861, the Ajawa tribe (Yao) were lying waste the country round Lake Nyasa and carrying off the inhabitants, the Manganja, as slaves. In their ascent of the Shiré, Livingstone and the UMCA missionaries encountered several of these cavalcades, drove off the slavers and freed the slaves.

whose hands were raw and blistered from hauling cables. They left the *Pioneer* thankfully at Chibisa's on 9 July 1861, and started the march up-country to find a mission site: 'a strange party', the Bishop wrote, 'Livingstone tramping along with a heavy, steady tread which kept one in mind that he had walked across Africa', the Bishop following with a loaded gun in one hand and his crozier in the other.

This moment in the Expedition's saga was later singled out by Livingstone as the summit of its fortunes. After so many tribulations, the way at last seemed clear ahead. Official backing, the healthy highlands found, a smiling country ('when will this fertile valley resound with the church-going bell?'), the mission with its splendid Bishop on its way and Mary Livingstone shortly due to rejoin her husband: the future looked bright. It was from this moment, however, that everything started to go wrong: slowly at first, then an avalanche of disaster ending in death for some and defeat for all.

The main reason was that old, ugly enemy, the slave-trade. Hitherto it had disgusted and spurred on the explorers, but they had never become directly involved. Theirs was the long-

In 1861 a party of missionaries was sent out by the Universities Mission to Central Africa, headed by an active young bishop, Charles Mackenzie. He had been consecrated at the Cape by Bishop Gray, whose official residence, Bishopscourt, is shown in this sketch.

term strategy of opening a way for the legitimate trade that
would supplant it, not the short-term tactic of driving off
slavers and rescuing their prey. A militant tribe called the
Ajawa (Yao) living near Mt Zomba, instigated by slave-
traders at Tete, had begun to raid into the Shiré valley, the
home of the Manganja tribe. They did not merely capture
people, they left a trail behind of burnt villages, pillaged crops,
orphaned children and rotting corpses. Few Englishmen, and
no Christian missionary, could turn aside from these sights like
the Pharisee and not, sooner or later, intervene. And interven-
tion must inevitably draw them into the quicksands of inter-
tribal war.

A week after the party left Chibisa's, a gang of yoked and
manacled slaves approached the village where they were
resting. Jaunty black drivers armed with muskets drove on the
captives, sounding notes on their long tin horns and marching
with an air of triumph. 'Shall we interfere?' the white men
asked each other. Livingstone reminded his companions that
Government property left at Tete might well be destroyed in
retaliation if they freed the slaves. But anger and compassion
were too strong; with open eyes they resolved to intervene.

'The instant the fellows [Ajawa raiders] caught a glimpse of
the English they darted off like mad into the forest. . . . Knives
were soon at work cutting the women and children loose.' The
men were most difficult to free because of the stout wooden
poles with forked ends into which their necks were fastened.
Luckily, the Bishop had a saw in his baggage and 'one by one
the men were sawed into freedom'. Soon the women were
cooking a meal over fires fed by the sawed-up slave poles.
There were eighty-four freed captives, who had been subjected
to cruel atrocities; one woman had seen her baby's brains
dashed out before her eyes. The gang's leader, who escaped
with the rest, turned out to be a former slave of Major Secard,
which clinched the matter, for Livingstone, of Portuguese
complicity, although he exonerated the Major himself from
any blame. One of those sawn into freedom was a boy named
Chuma, who will be heard of again.

The English party were jubilant. At last they had struck out
directly against the hated trade and saved eighty-four human
beings. In doing so, they had declared war against the slavers
and, indirectly, against the Portuguese; but the Bishop was
certain that Livingstone's decision had been right – 'surely all

will join in thanking God that we have such a fellow-countryman'.

From that time, July 1861, they freed all the slaves they came upon. Retaliation by the raiders was only a matter of time. When the smoke of burning huts and the screams of women warned them that a raid was taking place, 'the Bishop engaged us in fervent prayer, and on rising from our knees we saw a long line of Ajawa warriors', who shortly afterwards 'closed upon us with bloodthirsty fury' and were driven off by musket fire. 'Do not interfere in native quarrels', Livingstone had advised the Bishop; this was the consequence of disregarding his own advice.

A pleasant site for the mission was selected about sixty miles north-east of Chibisa's at Magomero, a promontory surrounded on three sides by a river and shaded by tall trees. Its altitude was lower than Livingstone thought desirable for the health of Europeans. However, the missionaries now had over a hundred freed slaves to look after and, if they moved further on, they would leave the Manganja at the mercy of the Ajawa. So soon they were cheerfully at work laying out a village, bringing up stores, building houses, starting a school. There Livingstone left them to make an exploration of Lake Nyasa. With him went Kirk and the surly Charles, whom 'even Bishop Mackenzie, who tried to like everyone, was obliged to confess that he had failed in that case, even after trying'.

A four-oared gig from the *Pioneer* was carried past the Murchison cataracts, paddled up the papyrus-fringed river above and, on 2 September 1861, entered Lake Nyasa. Never before had Livingstone seen such a densely populated and closely cultivated region as the lake shores. The people were excessively inquisitive; 'we have to pass the time', Kirk complained, 'as wild beasts in a show', peered at, encircled and commented upon, whether at meals or at prayer, even when washing – Livingstone, who hated being seen undressed, had to creep into the reeds. His white skin seemed to him unnatural – 'like blanched almonds, or white mice'.

If the Africans were on the whole friendly, the lake was not. Sudden storms gathered its waters into mountainous waves that all but overwhelmed their little gig. The heat was intense, and they were plagued by clouds of midges which the local people caught by night and pressed into cakes; 'one, an inch thick and as large as the blue bonnet of a Scotch ploughman,

OPPOSITE The Expedition's militant leader, wearing as ever his consul's cap, 'sawed into freedom' some of the slaves. Among them was the boy Chuma who became his personal servant and was with him at his death twelve years later.

Chibisa's village on the Shiré was until
the famine of 1862-3 a prosperous centre
where the Manganja people bartered food
for cloth, beads, razors and knives. This
was sketched by Charles Mellor, one of
the UMCA missionaries at the ill-fated
station at Magomero.

was offered to us; it was very dark in colour and tasted not unlike caviare, or salted locusts'.

The lake-shore population thinned out and yielded to a region where slavers had all but stripped the country of its inhabitants. The shores were littered with skeletons, there was no more cultivation and 'only a few fishermen now cower among the rocks'. There was no food to be bought. A party of Makololo carrying stores and cloth was marching along the shore parallel with the boat. They refused to go any further. Livingstone, determined as ever not to be thwarted, abandoned the boat and led them over the steep, rocky mountains that cupped the lake. They ran into a party of armed warriors who threatened them, and once more his calm saved their lives. They lost touch with the boat, and four days and nights almost without food and quite without shelter demoralised the men, most of whom fled into the hills. Only two were with him when he managed to reach the lakeside where the occupants of the boat found him. Storms, hunger and the collapse of Kirk with fever forced them to turn back. They had travelled five-sevenths of the way up the lake and reached Nkata Bay. Kirk summed up for them all: 'The inactivity and pains in the joints from the sun, the gradual emaciation, the fevers and starvation of that Nyasa journey combine to make it the hardest, most trying, and most disagreeable of all our journeys. It is the only one I have no pleasure in looking back on.'

They reached the *Pioneer* on 8 November 1861, 'in a very weak condition', just over three months after leaving her at Chibisa's. Although they had failed to circumnavigate and survey the lake as they had intended, Livingstone had, as usual, made valuable observations, and had unveiled, for the dismayed inspection of the world, the hitherto unrealised ravages and extent of the slave trade organised from Zanzibar. The Arabs had put dhows on the lake to transport slaves from its western shore and to link up with slave routes crossing what is now Tanzania to the coast. Whereas in 1859 there had been continuous cultivation and thriving villages, there was now a stretch of 120 miles devoid of any human being. The slaughter was appalling, and not one in ten of the captives, Livingstone calculated, survived to reach the journey's end.

Bishop Mackenzie was at Chibisa's and full of energy; he had twice taken action against the Ajawa and freed more slaves. Unexpectedly, a white man arrived in a canoe: another young

Early in 1862 HMS *Gorgon* reached
the Kongone with a brig, the *Hetty Ellen*,
carrying, in sections, the *Lady Nyassa*,
which Livingstone had commissioned
at a cost of £6,000. Here the brig
is discharging sections of the *Lady Nyassa*
into the *Pioneer* to take up the Zambesi.

missionary, Mr Burrup, who with two others had made his way from Quilemane to reinforce the Magomero team. He brought the news that HMS *Gorgon* was due shortly at the Kongone bringing his own wife, Mary Livingstone, the Bishop's elderly sister and her companion. The missionaries went back to Magomero while the explorers set out in the *Pioneer* for the Kongone. Twenty miles below Chibisa's, she stuck for five whole weeks on mudbanks in a malarial region, and as a result the first death took place among the Expedition's Europeans: a carpenter's mate lent by the Navy.

After further delays and troubles, they sighted HMS *Gorgon* on 30 January 1862. 'I have a steamship on the brig', semaphored the Captain. 'Welcome news', Livingstone signalled back. There was a second signal: 'Wife on board.' 'Accept my best thanks', was the reply. The steamship was the vessel Livingstone had commissioned, built at a cost of £6,000 from his own pocket, and named by him the *Lady Nyassa*. With her came the faithful Rae. 'His whole heart is set on serving you', Young wrote. 'If one man can be devoted to another, Rae is devoted to you.'

The *Lady Nyassa* had come out in sections and now these had to be loaded into the *Pioneer* and taken to Shupanga for reassembly. There was also a great quantity of stores. The task proved slow and difficult, and Livingstone himself was partly to blame. 'I have rarely, if ever, seen a man so easily led', wrote the paymaster of the *Gorgon*. He kept changing his mind about loading and unloading things and, although he toiled away himself, he lacked the authority to make others do the same. The result was chaotic. 'It was well enough when only an ox-wagon or a number of untutored Makololo were in question', his fellow-missionary James Stewart observed, 'but it seems to fail when brought in upon other minds who think as well as himself.' A seaman from the *Gorgon* recalled: 'He was a most retiring man, counting himself among the least, when indeed he was among the greatest.' Here, perhaps, lay the clue to his failure to give clear and precise orders to men he knew to be more knowledgeable than himself in technical matters.

But at least Mary was with him, reunited after three unhappy years. Homeless, lonely, still hard-pressed for money and left to cope single-handed with her children's education, it was no wonder that her religious faith had given way and she had been plunged into 'spiritual darkness'. Was it dispelled on the Zambesi? We do not know; but during her brief time there her faith in God's benevolence received another shattering blow. Captain Wilson of the *Gorgon* had volunteered to take the Bishop's sister and Mrs Burrup up the Shiré to join their menfolk. With Kirk as guide, and a detachment of bluejackets, they reached Chibisa's on 4 March 1862, to hear that the Bishop was dead, and Burrup desperately ill at Magomero. Kirk and Captain Wilson hurried to the mission but arrived to find that Burrup, too, had died. Wilson and Kirk nearly followed suit, literally staggering back to Chibisa's in the grip of acute fever, with another of the Magomero missionaries more dead than alive.

It was a tragic, broken party of survivors that made its way down-river and sailed away on 4 April 1862. 'This will hurt us all', Livingstone exclaimed when he heard the news, resting his head in his hands in the dimly-lit cabin of the *Pioneer* at Shupanga. He foresaw that support in England for the mission would be weakened, perhaps withdrawn, and his dream of a civilised Christian community arising in the Shiré highlands brought to nothing. The fruit that had seemed almost ready to be plucked had withered. That night he wrote in his journal: 'I will not swerve a hair's breadth from my work while life is spared.'

'This will hurt us all.'

There was a heavier blow to come. On 21 April Mary went down with fever and was moved from the *Pioneer* to the house at Shupanga. Her husband and Kirk applied their remedies in vain. She sank into a coma and on 27 April 1862, she died, at the age of forty-one. She was buried at Shupanga under a baobab tree.

The tragedy, he wrote in his journal, 'quite takes away my strength. I wept over her who well deserved many tears.' Oddly, in view of the fact that she had had two paralytic strokes, he wrote: 'she seemed so strong'. That he loved her deeply, despite the anguish he caused her, there can be no doubt. 'In our intercourse in private there was more than would be thought by some a decorous amount of merriment and play. I said to her a few days before her fatal illness, "we old bodies ought now to be more sober, and not play so much". "Oh no," she said, "you must always be as playful as you have always been; I would not like you to be as grave as some folks I have seen."'

'For the first time in my life,' he wrote, 'I feel willing to die.' He hoped his own grave would be 'in some far-off still deep

'On the right bank of the Zambesi lies the dust of her whose death changed all my future prospects.' Mary Livingstone died at Shupanga on 27 April 1862 and was buried under a baobab tree.

forest, where I might sleep sweetly till the resurrection morn'. Although he never doubted that they would meet again in the glorious presence of their God, he wrote in a letter: 'I feel as if I had lost all heart now. . . . I shall do my duty still, but it is with a darkened horizon that I shall set about it.' Lonelier and more withdrawn than ever, more gruff and unapproachable, the only outlet for his need for love lay in long and frequent letters to his children at home, especially to Agnes.

Assembly of the *Lady Nyassa*, which had been expected to take a few weeks, took nearly six months' strenuous toil. By the time she was ready, the waters of the Shiré had fallen, and they had to wait until January 1863, to move her. A whole year had been lost. Livingstone took the *Pioneer* to sea and, with his companions, sailed her to Johanna, one of the Comoro islands where there was a naval base and a British Consul to help him replenish supplies. Kirk had this comment to make: 'When the weather gets foul or anything begins to go wrong, it is well to give him a wide berth, most specially when he sings to himself. If it is "The Happy Land" – then look out for squalls and stand

152

clear. If "Scots wha hae" – then there is some grand vision of discovery before his mind. . . . But on all occasions humming of airs is a bad sign.'

Instead of returning straight to Shupanga, he decided in September 1862 to make another attempt to get up the Rovuma, though everyone else knew this to be a futile exercise. They found the river's level to be even lower than before. Nevertheless, up the river they must force their way in two whaleboats, with Kirk and Charles. Day after day the boats were dragged and shoved over mud-shoals, rocks and shallows. Kirk, who was dismayed by the whole adventure, observed: 'The infatuation which blinds him I cannot comprehend – getting boats jammed up a river where they cannot float and where it will soon be impossible to return. It seems madness. . . . I can come to no conclusion but that Dr L. is out of his mind.'

Before long, they were attacked by tribesmen who had guns as well as arrows – four musket-balls went through the sail of Livingstone's boat – and had to return the fire. To his great distress, Kirk killed a man. Even then, Livingstone would not listen to reason. 'Dr L. is a most unsafe leader. All he cares for is accomplishing his object at any risk whatever. It is useless

A photograph taken by Kirk in 1862 of the assembly at Shupanga of the *Lady Nyassa*; expected to take only a few weeks, the job took six months' hard work, and by the time it was finished the river had fallen too low to take the vessel up the Shiré until the following year.

making any remark to him.' This was the first sign – later there were to be many – that he had crossed that indeterminate border dividing the balanced from the obsessed. Nothing mattered to him now except refusal to surrender. Perhaps the truth was that he no longer really cared whether he lived or died, and his sense of responsibility towards those under his command had weakened almost to vanishing point. Long ago, he had decided that he would die in Africa – so he had told his Cambridge audience five years before – when God no longer needed his services. When and where that death took him seemed to matter less and less. But at last, amid 'a field of rocks' 156 miles from the river's mouth, even he desisted, and the boats made their way back. At least he had settled one point for good and all: like it or not, the only river route to Lake Nyasa was by way of the Zambesi.

Not until January 1863 did the *Pioneer* and the *Lady Nyassa* set out from Shupanga for Chibisa's, where the latter vessel had to be again dismantled and carried past the cataracts. It was a horrible journey. Less than three years before, the Shiré valley had been a land of milk and honey, thickly populated and well cultivated. Now:

'Dead bodies floated past us daily. . . .'

Dead bodies floated past us daily, and in the mornings the paddles had to be cleared of corpses caught by the floats during the night. . . . It made the heart ache to see the widespread desolation; the river-banks once so populous, all silent; the villages burned down, and an oppressive stillness reigning where formerly crowds of eager sellers appeared. . . . The sight and smell of dead bodies was everywhere. Many skeletons lay beside the path. . . . Ghastly living forms of boys and girls, with dull dead eyes, were crouching beside some of the huts.

Amid these grisly scenes, they progressed at the rate of half a mile a day. 'I pity the Dr more than I can say', wrote Horace Waller, one of the Magomero missionaries. 'The discontent and murmurs are sickening; it is a ship divided against itself, plank by plank.' On top of all this, the missionaries at Magomero were dying one by one and also running out of food, which prompted Richard Thornton, now back in the *Pioneer*, to volunteer to march overland and bring back sheep and goats from Tete. On his return, exhausted by a gruelling journey, he collapsed with fever and dysentery which he was too weak to overcome. So died the first – and youngest – of the original team. By then both Kirk and Charles were seriously ill from the same diseases, and Livingstone agreed to let them go.

It was now the leader's turn to become so seriously ill that for a month the faithful Kirk stayed on to nurse him. Then he and Charles departed in May 1863 leaving of the original six only Rae. It was by now obvious that the Expedition had run its course and must soon be recalled. In July, that recall reached the *Pioneer* in a fashion that Livingstone resented. A man sent on ahead from an approaching party which included Bishop Tozer to replace Mackenzie 'hailed the ship's company in strong Surrey dialect: "No more pay for you *Pioneer* chaps after December – we brings the letter as says it!"' The dispatch from the Foreign Secretary was couched in impeccable diplomatic phrases but came to the same thing.

The Expedition had lasted three times as long as had been planned, and cost a great deal more than three times as much. The orders were to deliver the *Pioneer* over to the Navy at the Kongone by the end of the year. Rather more than five months remained. Most men would have called it a day and started to move the stores and the two vessels down to the sea. But not Livingstone. He had, he reckoned, until early December, when the annual flooding of the river would make the downward passage easy, to put to a useful purpose. He resolved to spend the time in further exploration of the lake and its shores.

He had a boat from the *Pioneer* hauled past the Murchison cataracts but 'clumsy Shupanga men' capsized it in the river above, and his intention to sail up the lake had to be abandoned. He remained firm and proposed to go on without a single white companion. The others in the *Pioneer* demurred and managed to persuade him to take another European, so he picked 'the steward' on the grounds that the man had been ill and needed exercise. Nothing is more typical of Livingstone at this time than his omission even to mention the steward's name. This man trudged across 760 miles of unknown Africa, enduring in full measure the hardships and dangers, threatened by warriors of the militant Ngoni tribe (an offshoot of the Zulus), often hungry and sick, in total anonymity. 'The steward, having performed his part in the march right bravely', was the leader's only comment, 'rejoined his comrades stronger than he had ever been before.'

They left Chibisa's on 19 August 1863, walked up the lake as far as Kota-Kota and then struck westwards, climbing to a tableland 3,500 feet high where winds were bleak and one of the men died. This was a watershed, and the inhabitants told him of a large river further on which fed a lake they called Bemba (now Banguelu), and beyond that of another lake, Mwero, and another river, the Lualaba – always further on. He was hearing of the region where, ten years later, he was to die.

He turned back reluctantly and reached Chibisa's and the *Pioneer* on 1 November 1863. As soon as the river rose sufficiently, they set out for the coast to hand over to the Captain of HMS *Orestes*. With them went the *Lady Nyassa*, never to be launched on the lake of her name. With them also went some forty of the freed slaves who had been settled at the Magomero mission. For now the final and most hurtful blow of all had fallen. At least one concrete good had been achieved – Livingstone always discounted the importance of his geographical discoveries – and one of his aims, the most important, had been realised: the planting of the UMCA mission in the Shiré valley. Now this, too, collapsed. Bishop Tozer decided that Magomero was too unhealthy, and too much at the mercy of the slavers, to be maintained, and that the whole mission must be withdrawn to Zanzibar. Livingstone was too involved and too broken-hearted to accept the decision. In his view, the Bishop had ignominiously turned tail and fled, and with the departure of the missionaries went 'the last ray of hope for this down-trodden people'.

Two British cruisers were standing off the Kongone and they took the *Pioneer* and the *Lady Nyassa* in tow, and proceeded to Mozambique. On the way a cyclone hit them and only superb naval seamanship saved the two river vessels with all aboard, including the Magomero missionaries, from destruction. The little *Lady Nyassa* with her three-foot draught stood up so well to the savage buffeting that her owner decided to embark on one of the most remarkable, and quite the most unexpected, of his journeys. He wanted to sell the vessel, but not to the Portuguese who might use her to transport slaves. Failing to find a buyer in Zanzibar, he decided to sail her across the Indian Ocean to Bombay.

He took three naval ratings – a stoker, an ordinary seaman and a carpenter; seven 'Shupanga men' who had never been to sea in their lives; and two boys, one of whom was Chuma. He had intended to take Rae, but this staunch engineer accepted

A portrait of Chuma, the boy freed by the explorers on the Shiré, who became the Doctor's personal attendant and was the first to bring news of his master's death to the outside world.

the offer of a job on a sugar plantation in Johanna, where he died the following year. The seaman said 'there was something wrong with the engines' of the *Lady Nyassa*, but in any case they could not be used except in emergencies, for the skipper had shipped only fourteen tons of coal. And he had, he reckoned, eighteen days to get her to Bombay before the breaking of the south-west monsoon closed the ocean to sailing craft for two months. He was now aged fifty and looked more – 'very old and grey, and face wrinkled like a gridiron'.

Leaving Zanzibar on 1 May 1864, the vessel – almost a coracle, one would think, with her shallow draught – ran into adverse conditions: first contrary currents, and then for several weeks she was all but becalmed and could make only forty or fifty miles in twenty-four hours. Bilious fevers attacked the ratings and one of them staged a one-man mutiny which was quickly quelled. The Zambesians proved themselves 'capital sailors', learned to steer, and all were 'so eager to do their duty that only one of them lay down from sea-sickness during the whole voyage'.

Men for Sale

The slave trade in east and central Africa was in the hands of Arab and Swahili subjects of the Sultan of Zanzibar. To the island's great slave market trudged gangs of captives, yoked or chained together, from their distant villages. Livingstone reckoned that only one in ten survived. The slavers left a trail of burnt-out villages, pillaged crops and rotting corpses.

RIGHT Susi, one of Livingstone's personal attendants.
BELOW A slave-gang in Zanzibar.

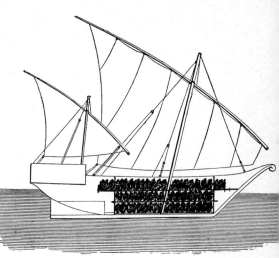

ABOVE The slaves were taken from Zanzibar in
dhows, the Arab sailing craft. The slaves were
packed below the deck to escape the vigilance of the
British Navy, operating anti-slavery patrols.
BELOW A native village raided by slavers.

'All ill-natured, and in this I am sorry to feel compelled to join', Livingstone entered in the log after three weeks of empty flapping sails, thunderclouds but no wind, dead calm all night. He grew depressed and brooded on his failure, on the weak-kneed conduct (as he still considered it) of Bishop Tozer, on his future, and on death which was seldom out of his mind. 'I shall have nothing to do at home; by the failure of the Universities Mission my work seems in vain. . . . Am I to be cut off before I can do something to effect permanent improvement in Africa?' But flying fish, sea-snakes, brightly coloured dolphins, a brown bird which 'bounds off the water like an India rubber ball', fed his unquenched thirst for observation. 'Incessant activity is a law in obtaining food. If it could be caught with ease and no warning given, races would have the balance tipped against them and carnivora alone prevail.'

At last breezes sprang up, but the vessel with her heavy screw proved to be so sluggish that 'it takes almost a gale to get $4\frac{1}{2}$ knots out of her'. They were running short of water, and the weather was breaking up before the imminent monsoon. Despite his inexperience at sea, the master could enter with confidence in his logbook their exact distance from Bombay. It was a queer log, breaking off from normal barometer and wind recordings to note with contempt a translation of two lines from Horace by Lord Ravensworth, adding: 'Pity he had nothing better to engage his powers, as for instance the translation of the Bible into some of the languages of the earth!'

On their forty-third day at sea they sighted land, 115 miles south of Bombay. Next morning, in a thick haze, he 'steered right into Bombay most thankfully. . . . No one came for a good while.' In his *Narrative* he recorded: 'We had sailed over 2,500 miles. The vessel was so small, that no one noticed our arrival.' When they did, everyone was kind. The Governor, Sir Bartle Frere, invited Livingstone to stay and the merchants encouraged him in his belief that cotton grown in Africa would find a profitable market. But he did not sell the *Lady Nyassa*. 'With the sale, which many seem ready to effect,' he wrote to Maclear, 'came the idea most vividly, "you thereby give up future work in Africa", and I could not do it.' He paid off his men, adding a generous bonus, had to borrow £133 for his own passage money, and on 24 June embarked for England, which he reached on 23 July 1864.

trees

400 paces

covered with trees

covered with trees

covered with trees

400 feet deep +

filled in N trees

Dry

150 paces

Trees

sides perpendicular
neck so narrow
one can see across
from + down to
N water

Victoria Falls – 1860 yards
wide – 310 feet deep – Garden island in
middle – blue line shews water flowing from
both ends to the escape –

7
Zanzibar
to
Ujiji

mbwo

ABOVE The grave of Archbishop Mackenzie at Malo Ruo,
by Charles Mellor, 22 January 1863.

PREVIOUS PAGES A page from Livingstone's notebook.

164

ON ARRIVAL IN LONDON, Livingstone called on the Murchisons and was swept off, just as he was, to a grand reception given by Lady Palmerston. She was 'very gracious – gave me tea herself'. Next day he got himself a dress suit and dined with Lord and Lady Dunmore; then on to the Duchess of Wellington's reception: 'A grand company – magnificent rooms –'; the ladies glittering with gems; elegant food, liveried servants. Much to his surprise, he was being lionised again. Not only was he too modest to expect acclaim but this time he was returning as a failure, at least in his own eyes. But it was only his particular purpose that had failed. The general object of the Expedition, as laid down in his instructions – to add to knowledge of the geography and resources of East and Central Africa – had most certainly been attained. And, as a man, he had set an example of courage and endurance in the face of overwhelming hardships that made his countrymen feel proud and grateful. He had sought no honours and no riches for himself, but only the good of humanity. So his unpolished manners, his difficult speech, his lack of social graces did not signify. No one expected a great explorer to look and behave like a tame poodle. He was a mastiff, but a gentle one when in the company of his compatriots.

At the Foreign Office his welcome was more reserved. Lord Russell was 'very cold, as all the Russells are'. This was scarcely surprising. For six years the Foreign Secretary had been bombarded by lengthy dispatches urging him to bully the Portuguese into drastic action against the slave-trade. For various reasons he would not go to the lengths Livingstone demanded. His Consul in Quilemane had become a most irritating thorn in his side. Now the thorn had at last been plucked out, he was not going to give it any encouragement.

Greatly as Livingstone disliked public speaking, he accepted an invitation to address the annual meeting of the British Association, and lashed out to an audience of 2,500 at Bath against the Portuguese and their connivance at the slave-trade. Outraged, the Portuguese hit back and accused him of trying to oust them from East Africa in favour of his own nation. Once again he had directed attention to Africa, and for the second time settled into the uncongenial task of writing a book to keep alive the interest he had aroused. First he went to Hamilton to visit his family which included the five-year-old daughter Anna Mary, a 'nice little girl', whom he had never

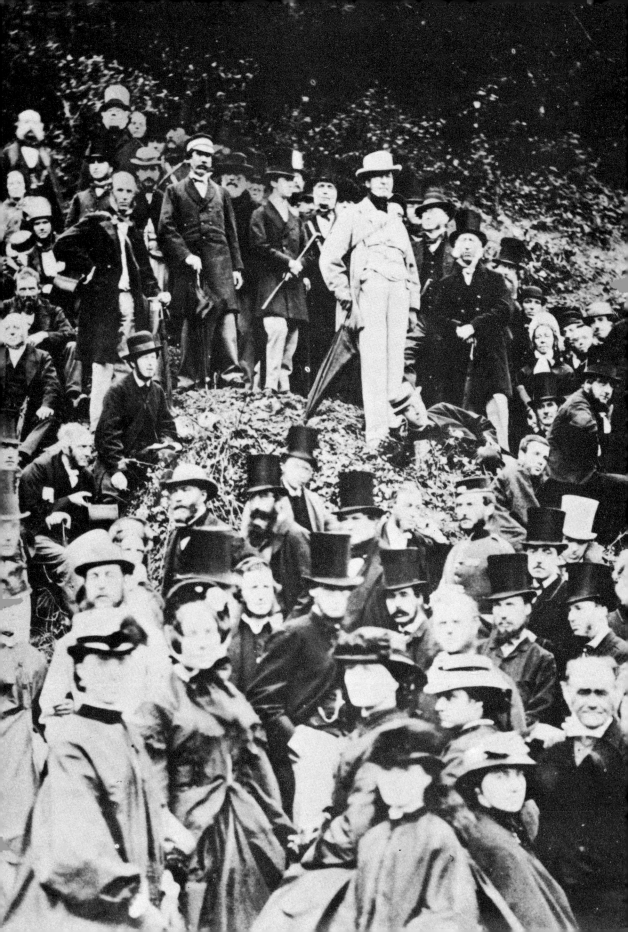

seen. He gave her a doll – a black one which she did not like.

Livingstone's tirelessness was as remarkable on paper as on the march. Not only were words poured without stint into his notebooks and journals but he kept up a vast correspondence with friends and acquaintances old and new: with Cabinet Ministers and his small children, with men of science like Murchison and Maclear and his former fellow-students at Ongar, now missionaries in all parts of the world; with dukes, bishops and old ladies who sent him presents. Now this industrious habit found its reward. Among the regular recipients of his letters were several rich, well-born sportsmen who had passed through Bechuanaland and whom he had sometimes been able to befriend: Oswell, of course, who had done more to befriend him, but also Varden, Steele and William Webb, whose seat was at Newstead Abbey near Nottingham. Livingstone had once rescued Webb when he was seriously ill in the bush and brought him to Kolobeng to recover. Now Webb invited Livingstone to Newstead, Byron's old home, for an indefinite stay.

Livingstone refused because he did not want to be parted from his daughter Agnes. The Webbs invited her too. He refused again because Agnes needed music lessons; that, said the Webbs, could be arranged with ease. Webb had a gay Irish wife and four young daughters, and lived the satisfying life of a well-to-do country squire. So Livingstone settled in to write his *Narrative of an Expedition to the Zambesi and Its Tributaries* and stayed for eight months, probably the happiest in his life since his wife's death, despite the toil of writing. At Newstead there was scope for the sense of fun and gaiety buried under that worn, austere appearance. The Webbs' famous guest took a frolicsome and even boisterous part in their simple country-house pleasures: charades, quadrilles and blind-man's-bluff at Christmas, nursery teas with clotted cream, duck-decoying on a pond. 'He was always extremely neat and careful in his appearance', a daughter of the house recalled, 'although there was nothing in the least clerical in his manner or dress.' Nor did the tribal customs of the English gentry disconcert him: the liveried servants, the carriages, grooms and gamekeepers, the dinner parties and socially eminent callers. 'He had naturally the hereditary good breeding of all Highlanders who, although in some cases they may have minor details of etiquette to learn, never have anything essential to unlearn.'

OPPOSITE In 1865 Livingstone addressed a packed meeting of the British Association for the Advancement of Science at Bath, presided over by Sir Roderick Murchison (centre). He used this platform to attack the Portuguese Government for its failure to do away with the slave trade in its East African domains.

There was talk, at this time, of public recognition – perhaps a CB or even KCB. Lord Palmerston sent a scout to Newstead to sound him out in the usual roundabout fashion. Was there anything the Prime Minister could do for him? Greatly, no doubt, to the scout's surprise, the answer was yes, certainly: a treaty with the Portuguese Government guaranteeing free access for all nations to the Shiré highlands. No honour was offered, nor did the Queen invite a further audience. He was not exactly in disgrace, but his attacks on Portugal had been blunt and embarrassing; the Prince Consort had been a cousin of the Portuguese King.

In order that his brother should enjoy the American royalties on his book, Livingstone linked Charles's name with his own on the title page. On 15 April 1865, he summoned Agnes to write FINIS. Although the freshness of his earlier work was lacking, it sold nearly five thousand copies on the day of publication and ten thousand in the first five weeks.

The question of the sources of the Nile was being hotly debated among geographers, following the recent discoveries of Burton, Speke and Baker. There were other controversies. Sir Roderick Murchison came to stay at Newstead, discussed it all with Livingstone and shortly afterwards wrote: 'There is at this moment a question of intense geographical interest to be settled; namely, the watershed, or watersheds, of South Africa.' Who could tackle this better than his old friend? 'I cannot believe you now think of anchoring for the rest of your life on the mud and sandbanks of England. Let me know your mind. . . .'

Livingstone's mind was quite clear. He was going back to Africa. 'I would not consent to go simply as a geographer', he wrote to James Young, 'but as a missionary, and do geography by the way.' His thoughts at this stage were turning back towards his first and true vocation, that of an itinerant preacher and healer. Encouraged by his response, Murchison persuaded the Royal Geographical Society to allocate £500, and the Government to match it, towards the cost of another expedition. James Young doubled the stake. By any standards, £2,000 was a very meagre sum to send even the least demanding of explorers into the depths of central Africa, probably for several years. But it was enough for Livingstone, who was counting on a substantial sum from the sale of the *Lady Nyassa*. He invited Kirk to join him, but Kirk was getting married and

Livingstone's youngest daughter, Anna Mary, born at Kuruman,
was five years old before he saw her. She was living with
his widowed mother and two sisters at Hamilton in Scotland.

While in Britain in 1865 Livingstone heard of the death in a prisoner-of-war camp in North Carolina, of his eldest son Robert Moffat (left), at the age of eighteen. Robert, estranged from his father, had joined the Federal army in the American Civil War.

OPPOSITE Among the young sportsmen on big game shooting safaris who visited the Livingstones in Bechuanaland was Major Frank Varden. The missionary kept alive his friendship by regular correspondence and was photographed with the Major when he visited England in 1857.

refused, going instead to Zanzibar first as medical officer and then, when the post fell vacant, as HM Consul. Charles also got a consulship, thanks to his brother's efforts, at Fernando Po.

In June, David heard that his mother was sinking and went to Hamilton, where news reached him of his eldest son's death from wounds, at the age of eighteen, in a prisoner-of-war camp in North Carolina. Robert's short life had not been happy. In his father's view, wild and undisciplined, a rebel against all authority, he had enlisted in the Federal Army under an assumed name to fight against slavery, as his father was doing in another field. David had scarcely seen his son and made in his journal one of those bald, seemingly heartless comments

OPPOSITE ABOVE In July 1863, the Zambesi Expedition heard the news of its recall at Chibisa's, the village of the Manganja chief just below the Murchison cataracts which had been their base for exploration of Lake Nyasa and for the ill-fated mission at Magomero.

BELOW At Shupanga, on the lower Zambesi, the Expedition had established a base for stores. Here the *Ma-Robert* and later the *Pioneer* were put together; and here Mary Livingstone died. When local chiefs came to call on Europeans, dances were often staged in their honour.

that strike so coldly on modern ears: 'Robert we shall never hear of again in this world, I fear; but the Lord is right and just and merciful in all His ways. He would hear the cry for mercy in the hospital at Salisbury.' No thought seems to have crossed his mind, or at any rate none found its way into his journal, that his own failure to provide a home for his family and care for his children might lie at the root of Robert's tragedy.

In mid-August 1865, he looked his last on England at Folkestone, *en route* for Paris where he left Agnes in a Protestant school. ('Avoid all nasty French novels', he advised her. 'They are very injurious, and have a lasting injury on the mind and heart.') Thence to Bombay, to sell the *Lady Nyassa* and collect men and stores. For the vessel he got only £2,300, little more than a third of what she had cost him; he invested the money in an Indian bank which failed within the year, and not a penny remained.

In Bombay he recruited ten Indian sepoys and nine young boys from a school for Africans freed from slave-ships by the Navy, situated at Nassick, outside the city. Two other lads, Chuma and Wikitani, whom he had freed himself from a slave-gang in 1861 (both Yaos), were waiting for him in Bombay, and two youths from Shupanga, Susi and Amodi, who been woodcutters for the *Pioneer*. In Zanzibar he added ten men from Johanna. There was also a small menagerie: water-buffaloes, most of which died in Zanzibar while he was waiting for a ship to take him to the Rovuma; six camels; two mules; four donkeys; and his favourite poodle, Chitane. The main purpose of the livestock was to test their susceptibility to tsetse-born disease on the mainland.

His small party disembarked at Mikindani on 24 March 1866. His year in England had restored his health and morale, and he was happy to be back in Africa.

The mere animal pleasure of travelling in a wild unexplored country is very great. When on lands of a couple of thousand feet elevation, brisk exercise imparts elasticity to the muscles, the mind works well, the eye is clear, the step is firm, and a day's exertion always makes the evening's repose thoroughly enjoyable. . . .

The effect of travel on a man whose heart is in the right place is that the mind is made more self-reliant; it becomes more confident of its own resources – there is greater presence of mind. The body is soon well-knit; the muscles of the limbs grow as hard as a board, and seem to have no fat; the countenance is bronzed, and there is no dyspepsia.

Last visit to Chibisa July 15. 1863

Katako. A native dance In honour of a chief visiting Shupanga, to

Livingstone's personal attendant Susi, who stuck to him through thick and thin and was with him when he died. Susi had been a woodcutter for the *Pioneer*.

Africa is a most wonderful country for appetite, and it is only when one gloats over marrow-bones or elephant's feet that indigestion is possible. No doubt much toil is involved, and fatigues of which travellers in the more temperate climes can form but a faint conception; but the sweat of one's brow is no longer a curse when one works for God; it proves a tonic to the system, and is actually a blessing. No one can truly appreciate the charm of repose unless he has undergone severe exertion.

Such words become ironic when read as a prelude to six years when animal pleasure, a clear eye and taut muscles were surrendered bit by bit to the gradual erosion of an ageing body by sickness, hunger and despair.

With an extra twenty-four porters to carry loads, the little expedition set out on 6 April 1866, along the Rovuma. They were making first for Lake Nyasa and then for all that unknown, unmapped country beyond which the great watershed, whose secrets Murchison had charged his friend to unravel, was presumed to lie. Even at this stage, he had at the back of his mind the belief that if – or rather, with God's grace, when – he could determine precisely the river system he had already probed, he would be able to settle the origins of the three great African rivers; the Zambesi, the Congo and above all, the Nile.

The camels were a failure from the start. A path had to be hacked for them through the forest, they were very slow and the sepoys treated them with callous cruelty. Soon they were covered with festering sores. Livingstone's journal makes it sadly plain that from the start he failed to exercise authority over his men. When they defied him, he seemed, for the first time in his life, prepared to surrender: 'I gave up annoying myself by seeing matters, though I felt certain the animals would all be killed.'

Livingstone wanted to find a route to Lake Nyasa that would avoid country controlled by the Portuguese, and took his brother, Kirk and a small party in whale-boats up the Rovuma river, now the border between Mozambique and Tanzania. But the river, as seen here, proved too shallow and they had to turn back.

Evening halt.

Before long they found themselves in the wake of slave-raiders and the all too familiar difficulties recurred. There was no food. The porters became so weak from hunger that they could scarcely stagger on. 'These are the little troubles of travelling, and scarce worth mentioning', was the comment. The sepoys beat one of the surviving camels to death with the butts of their muskets. 'I thought of going down disarming them all . . . but it is more trouble than profit, so I propose to start westwards. . . .' Again the note of defeat.

It had never been his way to issue peremptory orders, still less to enforce them by blows or the whip. He had relied on force of character and moral persuasion which had never failed before. They failed now. The 'Nassick boys' refused even to carry their own kit; all he did was to reproach them and then to increase their pay. In June the porters refused to go any further; he paid them off, and thenceforward had to hire men, when he could, from village to village. He brought himself at last to order the sepoys to carry light loads under threat of flogging. The effect of this soon wore off, and a sepoy who was carrying the tea threw nearly all of it away. Nothing happened but a note in the journal: 'I shall try to feel as charitably as I can in spite of it all.'

The gruesome trail of the slavers oppressed their spirits: corpses tied to trees or lying on the path, starving orphans cowering in fireless huts, 'village after village, and gardens all deserted'. He wrote to his son Thomas: 'I trudged it the whole way, and having no animal food save what turtle-doves and guinea-fowl we occasionally shot, I became like one of Pharaoh's lean kine.'

Owing to the raiders' devastations he turned south-west towards the southern tip of Lake Nyasa, hungry still and with the sepoys lagging behind. Near the town of a Yao chief – at least a thousand huts – he fell in with an Arab slave-trader who gave him flour and meat, 'extremely welcome to a famished man'. This was the first of many occasions when he was fed, helped without payment and restored to health by the very Arabs whose trade was of the devil: a case of hating the sin but loving the sinner indeed. Now they had reached a land of plenty, among the men who sold their fellows; cloth was abundant, food very dear. The sepoys got completely out of hand and Livingstone at last screwed himself up to the point of dismissing them, paying them off with sixty-six yards of calico and

OPPOSITE ABOVE On her slow progress up and down the Zambesi and the Shiré, frequent stops had to be made to cut wood for the *Ma-Robert*'s ever-hungry engines. Food would be bought from local tribesmen, grain pounded in a wooden mortar and the meal cooked out of doors.

BELOW One of the keenest pleasures of the Expedition's members was the hour of relaxation when darkness fell and the evening meal was taken in the open. This sketch was made on the Shiré river, where supplies were plentiful when Livingstone's party first went up in 1859; three years later, slavers left a trail of devastation in the formerly prosperous countryside.

arranging to send them back with a 'respectable Arab trader'.

When, on 8 August 1886, they reached Lake Nyasa, he felt as if he had come back to an old home and was exhilarated by a bathe in its waters. Hoping to hire an Arab dhow to cross the lake, he found 'the fear which the English have inspired in the Arab slave-traders is rather inconvenient. All flee from me as if I had the plague, and I cannot in consequence transmit letters to the coast, or get across the lake.' So he had to march along the mountainous eastern shore, up and down steep ridges, mapping the rivers as they struggled on. He ran out of ink, and made a good substitute 'from the juice of a berry, the colour of port wine when expressed', by adding a little ferri carb. ammon. Chitane's hair was turning red, the colour of most native dogs, who were seen off from the camp by this faithful and pugnacious poodle.

On 15 September, they reached the Shiré. 'Many hopes have been disappointed here. Far down on the right bank of the Zambesi lies the dust of her whose death changed all my future prospects; and now, instead of a check being given to the slave-trade by lawful commerce on the Lake, slave-dhows prosper!' There too lay Bishop Mackenzie, with whom had perished all hopes of spreading the Gospel. 'The silly abandonment of all the advantages of the Shiré route by the Bishop's successor I shall ever bitterly deplore, but all will come right some day, though I may not live to participate in the joy.'

By the heel of the Lake, the Johanna men walked off in a body, leaving their loads on the ground and reducing the party to eight surviving Nassick boys – one had died – and Chuma, Susi and Amoda. (Wikitani had stayed behind with his family near the Shiré.) With his usual habit of making the best of things, Livingstone remarked of the Johanna men: 'They have been such inveterate thieves that I am not sorry to get rid of them.' They had stolen cloth, beads, gunpowder, everything, and the headman Musa had shared the loot.

Musa was a rogue, and his subsequent behaviour must be briefly related. In Zanzibar, he convinced Consul Kirk, with a cleverly concocted story, that Livingstone had been murdered near the north end of Lake Nyasa. Flags were flown at half-mast, and in London obituary notices filled the newspapers. But a former lieutenant in HMS *Gorgon* who had taken the *Lady Nyassa* up the Shiré, Edward Young, remembered Musa as one of his crew, and as an inveterate thief and liar. He

The Arabs were skilled seamen and navigated their small sailing craft, the dhows, across the Indian Ocean according to the monsoons. In the 1850s they put dhows on Lake Nyasa to carry slaves across from the western shore.

disbelieved the story, and volunteered to go to Lake Nyasa and discover the truth. With the backing of Sir Roderick Murchison, a small steel boat was built, and within nine months of Musa's arrival in Zanzibar, she was afloat on Lake Nyasa, on 8 September 1867. Young had little difficulty in picking up Livingstone's trail south of the lake and disproving Musa's story. Soon afterwards, the first letters in the explorer's own hand to reach the outside world were brought to Zanzibar, nearly a year after they were written. They told in full the story of Musa's desertion, and the Sultan of Johanna sentenced him to eight months in irons.

By the time Young reached Lake Nyasa, Livingstone was five hundred miles away at the most westerly point of his zig-zagging journeys. In the last three months of 1866, he and his retinue, reduced to nine, climbed the Dedza plateau (in modern Zambia) and dropped down into the Loangwa valley. Rain, Mazitu (Angoni) raiders and constant hunger impeded them, and they could average only three or four hours' march a day. On the last day of the year, he wrote: 'It has not been as fruitful as I intended. Will try to do better in 1867, and be better – more gentle and loving. . . . Let all the sins of '66 be blotted out for Jesus' sake.'

They climbed the north-western wall of the Loangwa valley

A dishonest headman of a gang of men from the Comoro Islands deserted Livingstone at the south end of Lake Nyasa and, on reaching Zanzibar, spread the tale that he had been murdered. Lieutenant Edward Young, RN was sent by the Royal Geographical Society to investigate. He found the tale to be untrue and at a meeting of the Society at Burlington House, London, gave an account of his journey in January 1868.

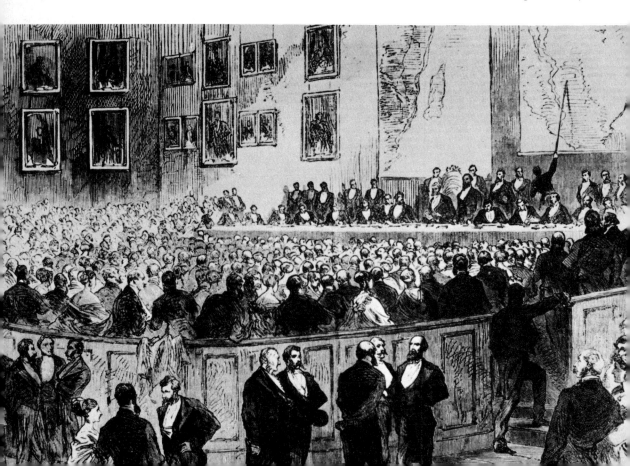

and the Machinga mountains, crossing deep ravines and trudging through forests of dripping bamboos that obscured the sunlight. 'The country is a succession of enormous waves, all covered with jungle, and no traces of paths.' Two falls by the man carrying the chronometers altered the instruments' rates and resulted, later on, in an error of about twenty miles in calculations of longitude. Hunger worsened; they gave thanks when they were able to buy a little stinking elephant meat in a village. Livingstone's constant companion was the poodle Chitane: 'on the march he took charge of the whole party, running to the front, and again to the rear, to see that all was right'. When crossing a flooded river, he was drowned.

It was a sad loss, followed by another which was a disaster. Livingstone had taken on two escaped slaves as temporary porters. He thought them reliable, but now they decamped in the middle of a forest, taking their loads. One had been carrying the load on which Livingstone's life literally depended: his medicine chest. 'I feel as if I had now received a sentence of

A steel boat was built, taken in sections up the Shiré, and assembled on Lake Nyasa, to enable Lieutenant Young to investigate the story of Livingstone's murder. By this time the explorer himself was some five hundred miles to the west, on the Lualaba river.

death', he wrote: as indeed, he had, although its execution was
to be delayed by six years. Yet nothing could happen except 'by
the permission of One who watches over us with tender care;
and this may turn out for the best by taking away a source of
suspicion among the more superstitious, charm-dreading
people further north'. Even to Livingstone, this must have
seemed a limp argument, for he added: 'It is difficult to say
from the heart "Thy will be done"; but I shall try . . . this loss of
the medicine-box gnaws at the heart terribly.' He made excuses
for the porters and trudged on through incessant rain, seldom
dry and suffering from 'real biting hunger and faintness' not
relieved by giant mushrooms which were 'good only for pro-
ducing dreams of the roast beef of bygone days. The saliva runs
from the mouth in these dreams, and the pillow is wet with it in
the morning.'

In this sorry state they came, at the end of January 1867, to
the Chambezi river, which by flowing into the Banguelu
marshes becomes one of the remote headwaters of the Congo.
Without knowing it, Livingstone had reached the immense
watershed of the Congo river system which he was to spend the
rest of his life attempting to unravel, suspecting it to be that of
the Nile. It is a complex system and the story of his wanderings
equally so. This is told, fully and memorably, in his *Last
Journals*, in which the tragedy of an unquenchable spirit in a
failing body is lightened by affectionate notes about the plants
and animals and native peoples as he went on his way.

Soon after crossing the Chambezi, they encountered a party
of Swahili traders heading for the coast, and for the first time he
was able to send out letters. The main Arab route to the interior
led from the coast opposite Zanzibar to Ujiji on Lake Tanganyika's eastern shore. He asked the Consul in Zanzibar to dispatch, to await him at Ujiji, some reliable porters and a fresh
supply of medicines, together with some coffee, soap and
candles, and a cheese in a tin, French preserved meat and half
a dozen bottles of port wine.

Despite attacks of rheumatic fever so severe that at times he
could scarcely walk, on 1 April 1867, he looked down on the
southern tip of Lake Tanganyika, nine years after the visit of
Burton and Speke. He found it, as they had done, of surpassing
beauty. Then he lapsed into unconsciousness, and it was nearly
a month before he was able to move. Instead of making for
Ujiji, where he would at least have been in touch with the out-

to get on. Had orders
who expected to be paid.
He replied that they
would return tomorrow.

Kantthumda
Nthunda to
Aunt.

Kasputu
N & a day N
to of Shuize

Marara

Thipita

10th Octr 1866 - March
1-5 N & then SW the
sepulchral grove one
tree called Bookwaiti &
no others else ...
+ 1h to Levise a fine
mountain torrent flowing
to Lake N & also we
ascended + 1 = 3 hours
+ 30 + 30 = 4 hours
Fine country lying in
long slopes with own
map streams at the
junction of two slopes

from point of nose to
up of tail 4 ft
throat - foot to knees 1-6

musk cat

side world, he decided to work his way up the western side of Tanganyika, a region that had not been visited by Europeans, to find out whether the lake narrowed. He still had frequent fainting fits as well as 'a constant singing in the ears and inability to do the simplest sum' – and he still had no drugs. And he heard that raiders were laying waste the country to the north-west of the lake. In making the decision to press on in that direction instead of to Ujiji, he seems to have crossed the dividing line between the intrepid and the foolhardy.

At Chitamba's, a village near the south end of the lake, he fell in with a large party of Arabs whose principal, Hamees, gave him food, beads, cloth and information. By now he had decided that if the way north was blocked by raiders, then he would go due west to look for Lake Mweru, of which he had heard in 1863. Lake Mweru, he believed, must form part of the 'central line of drainage' he was investigating, either of the Nile or of the Congo. This was the question, Nile or Congo, to which he was to seek an answer for the rest of his days.

He had to wait over three months at Chitamba's while the Arabs patched up a truce with a chief who had disputed their passage. Inactivity always chafed him, and he had nothing to read but Smith's *Bible Dictionary*. As the guest of Hamees, he was treated with unfailing courtesy. He watched wagtails nesting, took long walks in the sun to cure a swollen eyelid and saw slaves being bought and sold. 'Hamees advises patience.' At last, on 30 August 1867, his small party left Chitamba's in the company of the Arabs with a caravan of 450 carriers and slaves. It was not until 8 November that he stood, the first white man to do so, on the northern shore of Lake Mweru, through which the boundary between Zambia and Zaire now runs. From Arab and African sources he had pieced together a picture of this part. The Chambezi flowed into Lake Banguelu, out of it as the Luapula into Lake Mweru, and out of Lake Mweru, the River Lualaba flowed north-west into the unknown.

Instead of turning back for Ujiji, he decided to go on, with his six Nassick boys and Chuma, Susi and Amoda, to Casembe's near the southern end of Lake Mweru. It was in this region that the Portuguese Dr Lacerda, his one and only European predecessor, had died seventy years before. The current Casembe – the word means king or paramount – lived in savage style, his gateway ornamented by sixty human skulls, surrounded by subjects whose ears and hands had been cut off in punishment

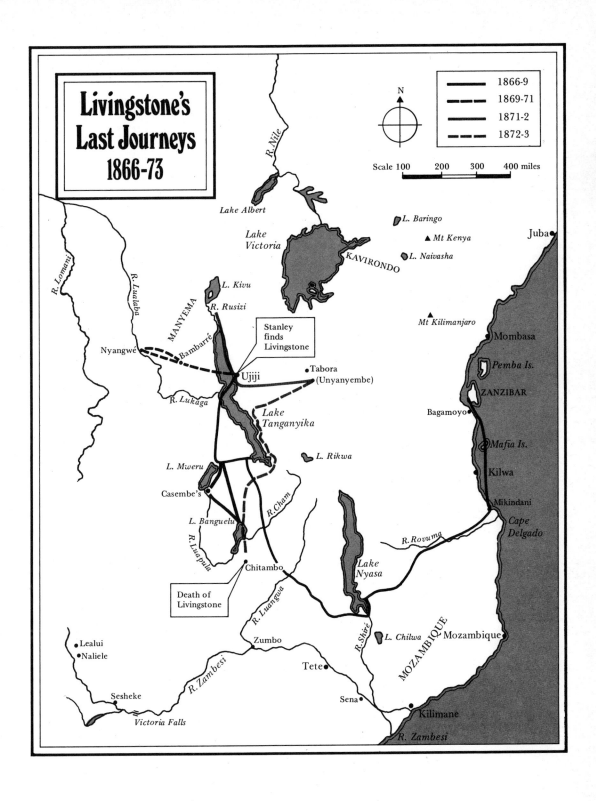

Livingstone's Last Journeys 1866-73

——	1866-9
– – –	1869-71
——	1871-2
– – –	1872-3

N

Scale 100   200   300   400 miles

R. Nile

Lake Albert

Lake Victoria

KAVIRONDO

L. Baringo

▲ Mt Kenya

L. Naivasha

Juba

R. Lomami

R. Lualaba

L. Kivu

R. Rusizi

MANYEMA

Nyangwé

Bambarré

Stanley finds Livingstone

Ujiji

Tabora (Unyanyembe)

▲ Mt Kilimanjaro

Mombasa

Pemba Is.

ZANZIBAR

Bagamoyo

Mafia Is.

R. Lukuga

Lake Tanganyika

L. Rikwa

Kilwa

Mikindani

L. Mweru

Casembe's

R. Cham

Cape Delgado

L. Banguelu

R. Luapula

R. Rovuma

Chitambo

Lake Nyasa

Death of Livingstone

R. Luangwa

R. Shiré

L. Chilwa

Mozambique

MOZAMBIQUE

Lealui

Naliele

Zumbo

Tete

Sena

Seseke

R. Zambesi

Kilimane

Victoria Falls

R. Zambesi

for breaches of etiquette. Here Livingstone found himself within striking distance of Lake Banguelu and wanted to go forward to see it; but the rains had started, and a note of weariness crept into his journal: 'I am so tired of exploration without a word from home or anywhere for two years, that I must go to Ujiji on Tanganyika for letters before doing anything else.' So back he splashed, squelched and waded, often waist-deep in water, shivering with cold and delayed by frequent attacks of fever and dysentery. 'One of my goats died and the other dried up. I long for others, for milk is the most strengthening food I can get.' It took him three months to retrace his steps only to find, by March 1868, that heavy rains had made the country towards Lake Tanganyika impassable, and the Arabs' departure was indefinitely postponed.

His journal suggests that, from about this time onwards, he became increasingly rudderless, at the mercy of events instead of controlling them. Now he decided to return to Casembe's and look for Lake Banguelu after all. At this point his followers rebelled, and he scarcely blamed them; 'they were tired of tramping and so verily was I'. Nevertheless he persuaded five out of the nine to change their minds (one subsequently absconded), and started out next day, 14 April 1868. Casembe provided guides, though he thought the whole idea a silly one – Banguelu was 'only water' after all; and on 18 July they reached the north shore of the great marshy lake. This was another major geographical find.

His intention was to hire a canoe and paddle across from north to south, investigating several populated islands on the way. All he had left to pay with was a single fathom of cloth. This the village headman accepted, and was rewarded by a talk on the Bible, on the evils of slavery and on 'what the Queen had done to encourage the growth of cotton on the Zambesi'. Only when embarked in a forty-five-foot-long canoe did he discover that his paddlers had stolen it from the inhabitants of one of the islands. They naturally refused to land there, and Livingstone got no further than an uninhabited island where he spent two cold, uncomfortable nights and 'dreamed that I had apartments in Milvert's hotel'. Next day they paddled back and Livingstone had nothing left to offer for the hire of another canoe except his coverlet; it had become very cold, and with great reluctance he had to retreat without making the exploration of the lake he had intended.

OPPOSITE At Casembe's, south of Lake Mweru, Livingstone visited a chief whose village gateway was decorated by sixty human skulls. This was a fairly common form of ornament in central Africa.

This was all the more frustrating because the belief had been hardening in his mind that this complicated network of rivers and lakes formed the ultimate headwaters of the Nile. 'If I am not deceived by the information I have received from various reliable sources,' he wrote with wishful thinking, for as geographers the Arabs, who were his sources, were anything but reliable, 'the springs of the Nile rise between 9° and 10° south latitude, or at least 400 or 500 miles south of the south end of Speke's lake [Victoria Nyanza] which he considered to be the sources of the Nile. Tanganyika is declared to send its water through north into Lake Chowambé or Baker's lake [Albert]; if this does not prove false, then Tanganyika is an extension of the Nile.' If it did not prove false, then in the stolen canoe he had been afloat on the birthplace of the river that had once concealed the infant Moses in its reeds. Then all would be worthwhile: 'the way seems opening up before me, and I am thankful'.

The way was closing, rather, thanks to the renewal of ferocious tribal wars. He could not get back to Casembe's. Rejoining the Arabs, he marched with them to Kabwabwata, near the north-east corner of Lake Mweru. Here there was another tedious delay while various Arabs converged upon the spot, from places as far afield as Katanga, to join forces for the march to Ujiji. The whole country was in a state of turmoil, and Bemba warriors who kept up an attack on the Arabs' camp for seven hours were driven off only with difficulty by the superiority of musket fire. On 11 December 1868, the caravan at last got under way: a party of Arabs, a long file of Manyamwezi porters, gangs of neck-yoked slaves carrying tusks and bars of copper, cattle and goats, and Livingstone's threadbare little band, now rejoined by the deserters whom he had forgiven. As usual he was optimistic. 'After trying the independent life they will behave better. . . . I have faults myself.'

On New Year's Day 1869, he wrote 'I have been wet times without number, but the wetting of yesterday was once too often.' He contracted acute pneumonia, coughed blood and fell delirious: 'I saw myself lying dead on the way to Ujiji, and all the letters I expected there useless.' His life was saved by the kindest of the Arabs, Mohamad Bogharib, who nursed him, gave him Arab medicines and had a litter made in which he was carried to Lake Tanganyika, reached on 14 February. During

An idealised etching of
Livingstone preaching to
the natives from H. G. Adams'
book of 1873.

the fortnight he waited for a canoe, lent by another Arab, to
take him across the lake, he squeezed twenty maggots from his
arms and legs. Another sixteen days' discomfort in the canoe –
emaciated, coughing, spitting blood, blistered by the sun –
brought him at long last to Ujiji on 14 March 1869. Here he
expected to find everything he craved for – medicines, milk,
decent food, rest, trade goods and, above everything, letters
from home.

At Ujiji there was practically nothing at all.

8 To the Ancient Fountains

PILFERING ON THE MARCH was a constant worry to all travellers; pilfering from unclaimed stores seven hundred miles from supervision, a virtual certainty. The medicines, wine and cheese were said to be at Unyanyembe (Tabora) about 150 miles eastwards. All the mail had vanished without trace. A few remnants of the stores and cloth were reluctantly produced and Livingstone 'found great benefit from the tea and coffee, and still more from flannel next to the skin'. An Arab supplied him with milk, he found a house and repaired it, and with his astonishing resilience started to mend. A fortnight after reaching Ujiji, he could walk half a mile, and shortly afterwards had finished writing forty-two letters. These he sewed into a canvas packet and gave to a Swahili trader, observing 'whether it will reach Zanzibar I am doubtful'. None of the letters was seen again. Although individual Arabs befriended him on the march, the Arabs in general, and even more their Swahili associates, rightly regarded him as an archenemy, and had no intention of allowing his ill reports of their activities to reach Zanzibar.

As soon as his health had so astonishingly recovered, he was anxious to be off again: not to Unyanyembe to retrieve his medicines, if indeed they were there, but once more westwards, to clinch, as he hoped, this matter of the sources of the Nile. He did not expect to be away for more than perhaps four or five months. Then he would return to Ujiji to collect the 'squad of men', medicines and stores which he had asked Kirk to send up from Zanzibar. Meanwhile, he would probe the country of the Manyema, said to be cannibals, west of Tanganyika, in search of 'an unvisited lake' with a river flowing from it northwards, which might be the Congo or might be the Nile. This river was the Lualaba, and it was the Lualaba he was now determined to reach.

Livingstone's refusal to accept defeat was matched by his refusal to admit a fact that denied an entrenched belief or thwarted a fixed purpose. The fact that he would not now admit was his absolute dependence on the Arabs. Formerly by travelling almost alone, almost unarmed, in peace and friendship, he had won the confidence of the fiercest African tribesmen and passed unscathed through regions where peace was unknown, strangers normally put to death and white men unheard-of. But the Africa he now had to deal with in the early seventies west of the Lakes was very different from his Africa of the

PREVIOUS PAGES Jacob Wainwright, one of the men recruited for Livingstone in Zanzibar by Stanley, accompanied the Doctor's remains to London and was a pall-bearer at his funeral.

Zambesi valley in the fifties. His arrival there coincided with a great expansion of Arab commerce. Hitherto, the Arabs and Swahilis had scarcely penetrated west of Lakes Nyasa and Tanganyika. Now, with their powerful armed caravans, they were thrusting westwards into virgin territory and returning with enormous quantities of ivory and coffles of slaves. In fact, a sort of ivory-rush was on, comparable in some ways with the gold-rushes of the Europeans. There was nothing civil or conciliatory about the behaviour of these caravans manned by the Arabs' slaves. They took what they wanted, took it brutally, and anyone who opposed them was killed or enslaved. In their bloody wake the native peoples were angry as a swarm of hornets, and no traveller was safe.

So Livingstone with his nine men had to travel under Arab protection, and at the Arabs' own time and pace. Attaching himself once more to the kindly Mohamed Bogharib, he set out from Ujiji on 12 July 1869. All went well as far as Bambarré, an Arab depot about a hundred miles to the west (in modern Rwanda). Bambarré was cold and wet and brought on attacks of malaria. While here, Livingstone mentioned a new trouble in a letter to his son Thomas: 'I am toothless, and in my second childhood.' He described how he had extracted his loose decaying teeth by fastening each one to a stump and striking the twine with a stick to jerk it out.

'I am toothless and in my second childhood.'

On 1 November he left the caravan and started with his nine men for the Lualaba, intending to buy a canoe and explore the river. After three weeks' march through dense, dripping forest they came to a tributary only twenty-five miles from its confluence with the Lualaba. Here 'all the people had been plundered, and some killed. . . . It was of no use trying to buy a canoe, for all were our enemies.' So, by 19 December, he was back at Bambarré, waiting for Mohamed Bogharib to march. On the 26th they started out in heavy rain, Livingstone suffering from fever and, a little further on, from 'choleraic symptoms'. They went due north, hoping to avoid the disturbed areas and 'to reach another part of the Lualaba and buy a canoe'. Six months later he was back at Bambarré, having failed a second time.

Once again he had left the caravan and for four months struggled on through wet forest, across flooded rivers, soaked by rain, getting progressively weaker from fever, dysentery and bleeding unrelieved by drugs. Yet in the midst of this he could write in his journal: 'Caught in a drenching rain, which made me fain to sit, exhausted as I was, under an umbrella for an hour trying to keep the trunk dry. As I sat in the rain a little tree-frog, about half an inch long, leaped on to a grassy leaf, and began a tune as loud as that of many birds, and very sweet; it was surprising to hear so much music out of so small a musician.'

Next morning, in a native hut, he had 'a delicious breakfast of sour goat's milk and porridge'. Rest, boiling the water and a new kind of potato 'soon put me to rights'. On 26 June 1870, there was the laconic entry: 'Now my people failed me; so, with only three attendants, Susi, Chuma and Gardner, I started off to the north-west for the Lualaba.' (The deserters went back to Bambarré where one of them, James, was subsequently killed and eaten by the Manyema.) Sickness, rain, mud 'too awful to be attempted', the brutality of the caravans – 'we passed through nine villages burned for a single string of beads' – and finally a new trouble, ulcers on the feet, defeated him. He limped into Bambarré on 22 July in great pain, with ulcers eating into bone and tendon. 'The wailing of slaves tortured with these sores is one of the night-sounds of a slave-camp.'

At Bambarré he was confined to his hut with these sores for eighty days, and only when he tried an Arab remedy – applying powdered malachite in water with a feather – did they begin to heal. He read the Bible through four times, and brooded on his quest, recalling legends of the founding of Meroe by Moses on the upper Nile, and Herodotus's speculations about the river's sources. Two passing Swahili traders told him of a spot in Katanga where four rivers rose, two to flow north, two south, with a remarkable mound in between. Might this not be the twin conical hills, Crophi and Mophi, mentioned by Herodotus? If he could only hire a canoe, he could reach Katanga up a tributary of the Lualaba. He was sick at heart as well as in body, 'in agony for news of home'. Almost as agonising was the wait for news of the 'squad of men' and stores that Kirk should have sent to Ujiji. Without these, he could not continue. 'To sit idle or give up before I finish my work are both intolerable; I cannot bear either, yet I am forced to remain by lack of people.' On New Year's Day 1871, he wrote: 'O Father! help me to finish this work to Thy honour . . . a caravan of 500 muskets is reported from the coast; it may bring me other men and goods.'

When the men at last arrived there were only ten of them,

and they had been the slaves of Indian merchants – the riff-raff of Zanzibar. They maintained that they had been sent to fetch Livingstone away, not to go forward with him, and immediately struck for higher pay. Nearly all the stores had been left behind at Ujiji. Nevertheless, he managed to get away from Bambarré with the quarrelsome and insolent slaves and his ever-faithful Susi, Chuma and Gardner, and on 29 March 1871, reached the goal. No white man had ever before penetrated so far into central Africa. The headman of the village at Nyangwé gave him shelter. The river, he thought, was getting on for two miles wide and it flowed 'away to the north' – towards 'Baker's Lake' and the Meroe of Moses on the Nile.

All he had to do now was to hire canoes, or even one canoe, and float down the broad river to prove or disprove his theories. But a canoe was not to be had for love or money. 'All flee from us', he wrote despairingly to Kirk. They were afraid that, once equipped with a canoe, he would raid the people across the river. The villagers kept promising a canoe, but none came. Yet he would not give up hope, and to while away the time visited the busy market where upwards of three thousand Manyema came to enjoy the day-long bartering, laughing and gossiping. Food was abundant, and 'little girls run about selling cups of water for a few small fishes to the half exhausted combatants. To me it was an amusing scene.'

July 15 was a fine morning and about fifteen hundred people came to market. It was a rule that guns were barred, and Livingstone was surprised to see three of the Arab Hassani Dungumbé's slaves with muskets. He watched the men bargaining for a fowl, and was walking away when shots were fired; then more shots; then panic. Men and women threw down their loads and ran towards the canoes on the river. The canoes jammed in the creek and the armed slaves, surrendering to blood-lust, poured their musket-balls into the crowd. It was a senseless, brutal massacre of hundreds of defenceless people. 'As I write, I hear the loud wails on the left bank over those who are there slain. . . . Oh, let Thy kingdom come! No one will ever know the exact loss on this bright sultry summer morning, it gave the impression of being in Hell.'

Despite the endless examples he had seen of callous human cruelty, this was too much. He had been forming a plan to cross the Lualaba with Dungumbé's caravan and march towards Katanga and the 'four fountains' with the mound between.

'It gave
the impression
of being
in Hell.'

'With these bloodhounds it is out of the question. I see nothing
for it but to go back to Ujiji for other men.' With his three faith-
fuls and the ten surly ex-slaves, he started on the 350-mile
tramp. 'All Dungumbé's people came to say good-bye.'

This was perhaps the worst of all his journeys until the last of
all. It was hard, rough going, he was scarcely ever free from
pain, sickness and bleeding, often hungry and increasingly
weak, and ambushed in the forest by Manyema. One spear
grazed his back, another missed him by inches. 'I felt as if dying
on my feet. Almost every step was in pain, the appetite failed,
and a little bit of meat caused violent diarroea. . . . All the
traders were returning successful; I alone had failed and
experienced worry, thwarting, baffling, when almost in sight of
the end towards which I strained.' On his last legs, he reached
Ujiji on 23 October 1871, 'a mere ruckle of bones'. A cruel
disappointment of the same kind as before awaited him.
The Swahili headman of the 'squad of men' sent up from
Zanzibar had stayed in Ujiji, sold all Livingstone's goods,
bought slaves and was living in style on the proceeds, often
drunk for a month at a time, and wholly unrepentant. 'He did
not leave a single yard of calico out of 3,000 nor a string of beads
out of 700 lbs.' Now truly destitute, only the kindness of another
Arab saved him from actual starvation. He had fallen among
thieves; but where was the good Samaritan?

He was close at hand. The most publicised meeting in African
history was about to take place. On the morning of 10 November 1871, 'Susi came running at the top of his speed and
gasped out, "An Englishman! I see him!" and off he darted to
meet him. The American flag at the head of a caravan told me
of the nationality of the stranger. Bales of goods, baths of tin,
huge kettles, cooking pots, tents, etc, made me think "This
must be a luxurious traveller, and not one at his wits' end like
me."' Henry Morton Stanley had arrived. No words ever fell
more sweetly on their hearer's ears than the famous greeting:
'Dr Livingstone, I presume.' Muskets fired, crowds gathered,
people cheered and even wept. Before long, Stanley was on the
straw mat covered with a goatskin which was the Doctor's seat
on his little mud-built veranda, pouring out news of all that had
been happening in the world – the opening of the Suez Canal,
the transatlantic cable, General Grant's election, the Franco-
Prussian war – while the worn, grey-bearded Doctor in his
faded blue cap and red-sleeved waistcoat, a bag with long-

Dear BRIAN'S WINTER reader,

Your opinion counts! Please answer the following questions and return this card after you've read the book.
There are no right or wrong answers. No postage is necessary, just drop the card in any mailbox.

Delacorte Press

1. Did you like this book? (Check one) ☒ It was great ☐ It was OK ☐ I didn't like it

2. Where did you first learn about this book? (Check one)
☒ Teacher ☐ Library ☐ Friend ☐ Other (Please specify) ☐ Magazine Ad ☐ Magazine Excerpt ☐ Direct Mail ☐ Bookstore (was it part of a display? Y/N __)

3. Which best describes you? (Check one) ☒ Student ☐ Teacher **(Skip to #13)** ☐ Librarian **(Skip to #16)** ☐ Other (Please specify) _____

4. Who picked this book? (Check one) ☒ I did ☐ Parent/Grandparent ☐ Teacher ☐ Librarian

5. Who paid for this book? (Check one) ☒ I did ☐ Parent/Grandparent ☐ Teacher ☐ Librarian

6. Was this book a gift? (Check one) ☐ Yes ☒ No

7. Will you recommend this book to a friend? (Check one) ☒ Definitely Yes ☑ *YES* ☐ Maybe ☐ Definitely Not

8. Would you read another book by Gary Paulsen? (Check one) ☒ Definitely Yes ☒ Maybe ☐ Definitely Not

9. In total, how many books have you read by Gary Paulsen? (Check One) *3*

10. Which of the following books, if any, have you read? (Check One) ☒ HATCHET ☐ THE RIVER ☐ NIGHTJOHN ☐ WORLD OF ADVENTURE TITLES.

11. How many books have you purchased for yourself (or were purchased for you) in the last 12 months? _____

12. Of the last 5 books you purchased (or were purchased for you) how many were for schoolwork? *1* **(Skip to #16)** last month? _____

13. How do you plan on using this book? (Check all that apply) ☐ Read aloud to class ☐ Add to classroom library
☐ Use in conjunction with HATCHET ☐ Recommend to colleagues ☑ Other (Please specify) *They buy them for us* ☐ Assign to individual students

14. Do you teach other Paulsen books in the classroom? (Check One) ☐ Yes ☐ No If yes, which one(s)? (please list) _____

15. Would you purchase class sets of this book if it were in paperback? (Check One) ☐ Yes ☐ No

16. Reader's name _____ Date of Birth ___/___/___ (Check one) ☐ Male ☐ Female

Address _____ City _____ State _____ Zip _____

BDD
Bantam Doubleday Dell
Books For Young Readers

BUSINESS REPLY MAIL

FIRST CLASS MAIL   PERMIT NO. 01239   New York, NY

POSTAGE WILL BE PAID BY ADDRESSEE

BANTAM DOUBLEDAY DELL
BOOKS FOR YOUNG READERS
AUTHOR MARKETING
1540 Broadway
New York NY 10109–1225

James Gordon Bennett Jr., proprietor of the *New York Herald*, who summoned his reporter Stanley to his hotel bedroom in Paris at eight in the morning and told him: 'Find Livingstone'.

awaited family letters on his knee, listened in wonder and began to speak of unknown places – Manyema, Casembe's, Mweru, Nyangwe – in his quiet tones. Stanley had forgotten nothing – even two silver goblets and a bottle of champagne to toast the Doctor's health and his own triumph.

This was in every way a most extraordinary meeting. Extraordinary in that it should have happened at all, against all the odds of timing and geography. And extraordinary in that when it did, these two men, such poles apart in age, in outlook, in character, in aim, should have found such pleasure in each other's company, and enjoyed four months of close companionship in harmony and even intimacy. This despite all Livingstone's reserve and solitary habit, his rejection of the values Stanley stood for, and despite Stanley's ebullient brashness. It was almost like love at first sight.

That Stanley should revere the older man was natural; the Doctor had by now become a legendary figure, and here was the living saint who was also a gentle, generous, sympathetic, even humorous old man, treating the young American journalist with a courtesy and sometimes a deference that touched his heart. Beneath the shell of a hard-boiled, go-getting, roving reporter for the *New York Herald*, Stanley had a heart to touch, and so his four months' association with Livingstone was not just a splendid chance to gather copy but a great spiritual experience, the turning-point of his life.

The first reactions of both men to the meeting were typical. Stanley was cock-a-hoop – had he not scooped the world in 'finding' the lost explorer? – and fascinated by this old, sick man so full of patience and wisdom, a sort of *guru*. Livingstone's reaction to being 'found' was simply a surprised gratitude that anyone, and especially the unknown American newspaper proprietor James Gordon Bennett, Jnr., should have gone to such trouble and expense on his account and sent him so many welcome presents. 'I am not of a demonstrative turn; as cold, indeed, as we islanders are usually reputed to be; but this disinterested kindness of Mr Bennett, so nobly carried into effect by Mr Stanley, was simply overwhelming. I really do feel extremely grateful, and at the same time I am a little ashamed at not being more worthy of the generosity.' It really did not occur to him that any motive save that of sheer disinterested human kindness could have lain behind Bennett's dispatch of his ace reporter, with no expense spared, into darkest Africa; and Stanley understandably did not enlighten him.

Different as these two seemed to be, they had more in common than met the eye. Both came from the humblest possible origins and had risen by their own determined efforts. The difference was that although Livingstone's origins were poor and humble they were respectable and kindly: in his boyhood he had never lacked love and care. Stanley was one of the rejected, his upbringing the most harsh and loveless it is

The Famous Meeting

'An Englishman! I see him!' Susi cried excitedly when Stanley's caravan reached Ujiji on 10 November 1871. Stanley had 'found' Livingstone; but the Doctor did not consider himself to be lost. He was, however, sick and destitute, living on the charity of the Arabs, and disappointed in his hope of finding at Ujiji stores and medicines that had been sent up from Zanzibar, but plundered by Swahili traders.

BELOW Livingstone's house at Ujiji, from a sketch by Stanley. It was here that Stanley brought the long-awaited letters from home and news of the outside world of which Livingstone had heard nothing since setting out from Zanzibar five and a half years before.

ABOVE The end of the search by Stanley for Livingstone.

LEFT The two men formed an instant friendship. Six days after Stanley's arrival they set out in a canoe to explore the northern end of Lake Tanganyika to find whether an outlet linked it with the headwater of the Nile.

201

possible to imagine. Born in 1841 in North Wales, the illegitimate son of a servant-girl and a ploughman, John Rowlands, he was abandoned in an orphanage that might have come straight out of the grimmest pages of Dickens. In charge was a sadist who ultimately went off his head, and in the meantime inflicted torments with the rod on top of those arising from cold, semi-starvation, humiliation and everything horrible that can be imagined under the mid-nineteenth-century poor-laws in a remote part of Wales.

The Welsh-American adventurer and the Scots missionary had in common qualities of extreme toughness, physical courage, inflexibility of purpose, pertinacity and a stubborn refusal to be beat. They shared, also, if to a very different degree, the same basic beliefs in Christianity and the role of their own civilisation in Africa. Of course there was a world of difference in their approach and outlook. Stanley fought his way through an obstacle, the older man tried patiently to inch his way round.

Livingstone observed in Stanley a generosity others did not always find. 'He laid all he had at my service, divided his clothes in two heaps and pressed one heap upon me; then his medicine chest; then his goods and everything he had; and to coax my appetite often cooked dainty dishes with his own hand.' With this treatment the sick and worn-out man made the last of his astonishing recoveries. He put on weight and grew almost plump. In fact it was Stanley who was the more often sick with bad attacks of fever. It was not only Stanley's medicine chest and good food but his companionship, after six years of loneliness, that proved so therapeutic. And there were letters from his children, from his friends – even copies of *Punch*.

Only six days after Stanley's arrival, the two men set out in a canoe to explore the northern end of Lake Tanganyika. Livingstone wanted to discover whether the River Lusizé flowed out of it, as the Arabs declared, although none of them had seen it. If they were right, then the Lusizé might flow on to enter Lake Albert and so to feed the Nile. But the Arabs were wrong; the river flowed into Lake Tanganyika and not out of it, and could have no connection with 'Baker's Lake'. There must be an outlet somewhere, Livingstone reasoned, even if they had not found it, and he suspended judgment. It was found two years later by Verney Lovett Cameron, emerging from a swamp on the western side to meander into the Lualaba and so, eventually, to feed the Congo and not the Nile.

Back in Ujiji, they prepared to start together for Unyanyembe where Livingstone would collect his stores and letters, and hire porters to go back and 'complete his work'. He was deaf to Stanley's entreaties to go with him down to Zanzibar and then home to rest, recuperate and at least get a set of false teeth. 'My judgment said, "all your friends will wish you to make a complete work of the exploration of the sources of the Nile before you retire."' One friend in particular: Sir Roderick Murchison. Livingstone had made him a promise, and that promise must be kept. To go back now, with the great question still unsettled, would be to admit defeat. At bottom it was Livingstone's pride, or at least his self-respect, that was the real issue. Jesus Himself had made it quite plain: 'No man, having put his hand to the plough, and looking back, is fit for the kingdom of God.'

After a journey of seven weeks, the two men with their retinues reached Unyanyembe on 18 February 1872. For the third time, Livingstone found that his stores had been plundered, though not completely; four flannel shirts were there from Agnes, and from Waller two good pairs of English boots. Stanley more than made up the losses from his own stores. But no porters were to be had. There was nothing for it but for Stanley to go down to the coast, recruit fifty good men – not ex-slaves – in Zanzibar, and send them back at top speed to Unyanyembe. He left on 14 March 1872. It was an emotional parting for them both. 'I feel as though I would rebel against the fate that drives me from him', Stanley wrote. 'My days seem to have been spent in an Elysian field.' They breakfasted together silently and neither could eat. After they had walked a little way together, Livingstone turned back. 'March!' Stanley cried fiercely to his men. 'I shall show them such marching as will make them remember me.' The Doctor never set eyes on a white man again.

The young journalist – thirty-two years separated their ages – never forgot this man who in four months had become to him an ideal version of the father he had never known:

His gentleness never forsakes him; his hopefulness never deserts him. No harassing anxieties, distraction of mind, long separation from home and kindred, can make him complain. He thinks "all will

Stanley was snubbed and derided by the stuffier British scientists who resented the speed and success with which he had found Livingstone, while they had merely talked of doing so. Stanley was deeply hurt, but settled down to write 'How I Found Livingstone', whose title did nothing to redeem his offence.

203

come out right at last," he has such faith in the goodness of Providence. . . . To the stern dictates of duty, alone, has he sacrificed his home and ease. . . . His is the Spartan heroism, the inflexibility of the Roman, the enduring resolution of the Anglo-Saxon – never to relinquish his work, though his heart yearns for home; never to surrender his obligations until he can write FINIS to his work.

There is a good-natured *abandon* about Livingstone which was not lost on me. Whenever he began to laugh, there was a contagion about it, that compelled me to imitate him. It was such a laugh as Herr Teufelsdrockh's – a laugh of the whole man from head to foot. If he told a story, he related it in such a way as to convince one of its truthfulness; his face was so lit up by the sly fun it contained. . . . Underneath that well-worn exterior lay an endless fund of high spirits and inexhaustible humour; that rugged frame of his enclosed a young and most exuberant soul. Every day I heard innumerable jokes and pleasant anecdotes. . . .

This unusual glimpse of high spirits and a bubbling sense of fun makes it clear that in Stanley's company the Doctor was unusually happy. Stanley's final verdict was: 'For four months and four days I lived with him in the same house, or in the same boat, or in the same tent, and I never found a fault in him. I am a man of quick temper, and often without sufficient cause, I daresay, have broken ties of friendship; but with Livingstone I never had cause for resentment, but each day's life with him added to my admiration.'

Five days after parting with Stanley, Livingstone marked his fifty-ninth birthday in his journal with this poignant prayer:

Birthday. My Jesus, my King, my Life, my All; I again dedicate my whole self to Thee. Accept me and grant, O Gracious Father, that ere this year is gone I may finish my task. In Jesus' name I ask it. Amen, so let it be. *David Livingstone.*

A tedious, depressing five months at Unyanyembe followed, waiting for the men from Zanzibar. He filled the days as best he could; tarring a tent, making cheese, doctoring Arabs, worrying about Herodotus and the Nile; observing a hen whydah bird rearing an orphaned family of ten: 'nature is full of enjoyment'. But he was awakened sometimes by dreams of slaving scenes that made him 'start up at dead of night horrified by their vividness'. On 1 May 1872, he finished a letter to the *New York Herald* with the famous sentence that was to be engraved on his tombstone: 'All I can say in my solitude is, may Heaven's rich blessing come down on everyone – American,

English, Turk – who will help to heal this Open Sore of the World.'

Just five months after Stanley's departure, the porters arrived: good, sturdy men, the best the Doctor ever had. This time he intended to approach the Lualaba from the south. He would go to the southern end of Lake Tanganyika, then south-west to Lake Banguelu, cross the Chambezi, skirt the southern side of the great marshy lake, then 'due west to the ancient fountains' in Katanga. 'This route will serve to certify that no other sources of the Nile can come from the south without being seen by me.' Then he would turn north to rejoin his old route on the upper Lualaba, and follow it down to that still unvisited Lake Chowambé, possibly the same as Baker's Lake Albert – 'which, I think,' he had told Stanley, 'will solve the whole problem'.

The only way Livingstone could get accounts of his journeys to the outside world was by sewing his journals and letters into a canvas bag and entrusting it to traders bound for the coast. This packet was carried by Stanley.

Chuma (left) and Susi
marched to Zanzibar with
Livingstone's embalmed
body, and later were brought
to England to be lionised.

'I know too much to be positive', he wrote while at
Unyanyembe. 'I am not even now at all "cock-sure" that I have
not been following down what may after all be the Congo.'
And in his journal he had written: 'I am oppressed with the
apprehension that after all it may turn out that I have been
following the Congo; and who would risk being put into a
cannibal pot, and converted into a black man for it?'

On 25 August 1872, the caravan, consisting of porters carrying fifty-pound loads, the five stalwarts Susi, Chuma and
Amoda who had been with him since 1864 and the former
'Nassick boys', Gardner and Mbruki, who had joined in 1866,
with ten head of cattle and two donkeys, marched out of

Unyanyembe. (There was also Amoda's wife Halimah, the leader's cook.) In his optimism, Livingstone hoped that six or seven months would settle the question, and then he would be ready to retire.

Within a month, the familiar entries started in his journal: 'Ill.' 'Ill with bowels, having eaten nothing for eight days.' The respite was over. 'Rest here, as the complaint does not yield to medicine or time.' Nor did his optimism yield to reality. 'I begin to eat now, which is a favourable symptom.' 'I am getting better slowly.' At least he was happy with the men sent by Stanley. They 'behaved as well as the Makololo. I cannot award them higher praise.'

In October they saw Lake Tanganyika a thousand feet below them, transformed by sunset into a sea of reddish gold. In November they were slithering in constant rain along muddy paths and going hungry in country pillaged by slavers. At the start of 1873 they were approaching Lake Banguelu at the worst time of year when rivers were in flood and the whole country inundated. The lake was, and is, a huge, leech-infested morass interspersed by channels of deep water with strong currents in which a man could easily sink and drown. All around were 'sponges', as Livingstone called them, or 'oozes': stretches of coarse, tussocky reeds and aquatic plants into which the traveller sank to his knees or deeper, spurted with squelching black mud.

From cheerless camps in the marshes, he wrote many letters home, although he had no way of sending them; they helped to dull the ache of loneliness. To his brother John in Canada, whom he had not seen for thirty years, he re-affirmed as his central purpose the ending of the slave-trade, and added: 'The Nile sources are valuable to me only as a means of enabling me to open my mouth with power among men. . . . Men may think I covet fame, but I make it a rule never to read aught written in my praise.' These words suggest that doubts about his fundamental belief, that he was engaged upon God's work, had begun to creep in. On the Zambesi, in the Shiré highlands, he had indeed been opening a way for the entry of Christianity and the ending of the slave-trade. But looking for the sources of the Nile – did that really contribute towards these avowed aims? Had not a worm of personal ambition, after all, entered in? His argument that he would speak with greater authority if he could solve the geographical riddle was plainly a feeble one:

his voice had plenty of authority already. Suppressing these doubts, he wrote to his oldest surviving friend, James Young: 'During a large part of this journey I had a strong presentiment that I should never live to finish it. It is weakened now, as I seem to see the end towards which I have been striving looming in the distance.' In the distance still. But beyond it lay rest, peace, his family. To Horace Waller: 'Will you speak to a dentist about a speedy fitting of artificial teeth? And will you secure some lodgings – say, anywhere near Regent's Park. . . . Agnes will come up, and will need accommodation at the same place.'

'I must plod on.'

Such dreams helped to sustain him in this world of pain and water. 'Rain, rain, rain, as if it never tired on this watershed. . . . I must plod on.' So weak was he that his men had to carry him across the rivers on their shoulders, the water often up to their chins. 'Each time I was lifted off bodily and put on another pair of stout willing shoulders, and fifty yards put them out of breath: no wonder! It was sore on the women folk of our party. . . . The water was cold, and so was the wind. . . . The Lake is near, but we are not sure of provisions. . . . Our progress is distressingly slow. Wet, wet, wet; sloppy weather truly, and no observations.' All this time the bleeding continued, and he clung to the theory he must have known in his heart to be absurd: 'I lose much blood, but it is a safety-valve for me, and I have no fever or other ailments.'

For the first time in all his wanderings, he was lost. The principal cause was not his own confusion but the accident to his chronometers that had occurred five years before, throwing out his longitudes by some twenty or thirty miles. Thus he thought that he was further to the west, and therefore nearer to the lake, than he really was. To make matters worse, a small fault in his sextant had developed without his realising it, and when he was able to make observations, these tended to increase the error. His only course was now to get canoes in which to cross to the south side of the lake. The problem was to find the chief Matipa, said to possess canoes large enough for such a large party. In this flat, featureless country they could pass within a mile of a village without seeing it, and entries like 'a drizzly night was followed by a morning of cold wet fog' show the conditions.

While immobilised by 'an excessive haemorrhic discharge', he was furiously attacked by red driver ants. 'I lighted a candle, and remembering Dr van der Kemp's idea that no animal will attack man unprovoked, I lay still. The first came on my foot quietly, then some began to bite between the toes, then the larger ones swarmed over the foot and bit it furiously, and made the blood start.' Dr van der Kemp could not have been more wrong. Driven from his tent, his 'whole person was instantly covered as close as smallpox (not confluent) on a patient'. These attacks are extremely painful, like being pricked continuously all over by red hot needles, and cause panic as well as pain. It was two hours before Livingstone was clear, yet he had the self-possession to observe: 'they insert the sharp incurved mandible, and then with six legs push their bodies round so as to force the points by lever power'. In this manner, 'they took all my fat', and it was not until late the following afternoon that 'they retired to enjoy the fruits of their raid'.

'Without canoes no movement can be made in any direction, for it is water everywhere, water above and water below.' Where was Matipa? On an island, but the island could not be found. 'I was ill all yesterday, but escape fever by haemorrhage. . . . I was never in such misty cloudy weather in Africa.' At last Susi and Chuma found Matipa and returned with a favourable reply. 'I am devoutly thankful to the Giver of all for favouring me so far, and hope that He may continue His kind aid.' But the canoes failed to come, and Livingstone led his unfortunate party through the swamp, sleeping on a 'miserable dirty fishy island; all are damp' and reaching Matipa's island on 3 March.

Matipa proved to be 'an old man, slow of tongue, and self-possessed', who for five coils of copper agreed to send them to the south side of the lake. But like most African chiefs, Matipa was in no hurry, and probably thought this sick, grey-bearded old white man was mad, wishing to travel for no apparent purpose in the rain. Meanwhile, there were drummers for entertainment, plenty of fish in the lake and plenty of beer. 'His wife is making *pombé*, and will drown all his cares, but mine increase and plague me.' For three weeks, frustration followed on frustration. Matipa 'promises everything and does nothing; nothing; the delay is most trying; Matipa is acting the villain, and my men are afraid of him.' On 19 March, his sixtieth birthday, the desperate traveller wrote: 'Thanks to the Almighty Preserver of men for sparing me thus far on the journey of life. Can I hope for ultimate success? So many obstacles have arisen. Let not Satan prevail over me, Oh! my good Lord Jesus.'

At last he could bear it no longer and, with some of his men, took possession of the chief's house and village, firing his pistol through the roof; Matipa fled. Within an hour or so, several canoes appeared. Livingstone's patience and goodwill were inexhaustible. Instead of berating the chief, he 'explained our delays, and our desire to complete our work and meet Baker', and embarked his party in four canoes on 24 March 'first giving him a present that no blame should follow me'.

It was wetter, if possible, than ever; everything was soaked, Livingstone's bed was put into the bilge, it was bitterly cold and they slept on a windswept, sodden island. The health of a robust young man might well have broken on such treatment; no old, sick man with chronic intestinal bleeding, even Livingstone, could survive. 'Nothing earthly will make me give up my work in despair', he wrote in the journal in a hand that was beginning to waver. 'I encourage myself in the Lord my God, and go forward.'

On 26 March they crossed the Chambezi. A canoe capsized and a girl, Amoda's, was drowned. 'A lion roars nightly. The fish-hawk utters his weird voice in the morning, as if he lifted up to a friend. . . .' Despite his desperate plight and the urge at all costs to go forward, Livingstone halted the party for five days on the south bank while he sent cloth back to Matipa to pay for a broken canoe. It was still raining. On 5 April they started off again, the goods and the leader in canoes, the men on land, or more correctly on marsh and mud. Livingstone's canoe was separated from the others; he slept in the open on an ant-hill. 'A lion had wandered into this world of water and ant-hills, and roared night and morning, as if very much disgusted; we could sympathise with him!' Next day the canoe kept sticking in the tangled mat of vegetation and they hauled it along by hand for almost every inch of the way. 'My men were all done up.' As to their leader, it is impossible to imagine why he was still alive. 'I am pale, bloodless and weak from bleeding profusely ever since 31st March, an artery gives off a copious stream, and takes away my strength. . . . Oh, how I long to be permitted by the Over Power to finish my work.' If he could only reach dry land on the south side of this interminable swamp-cum-lake, he still believed he could veer west, hit off the Luapula river and paddle down to the threshold of Katanga, and so to the 'four fountains' and the completion of his work.

On 13 April he noted that the sky was clearing, the wind dropping and 'it is the dry season well begun'. With a portable rain-gauge he was still meticulously measuring the daily fall, which was higher than had been observed anywhere else on his journeys. Despite his extreme weakness, he could still chronicle the scene around him with freshness and affection. 'The young of fish swarm, and bob in and out from the leaves. A species of soft moss grows on most plants, and seems to be good fodder for fishes, fitted by hooked or turned-up noses to guide it into their maws.' On the 17th another storm 'burst all our now rotten tents to shreds', and next day he was 'very ill at night, but remembered that the bleeding and most other ailments in this land are forms of fever' and took quinine. He mounted a donkey, and on the 19th recorded one of the greatest under-statements of all time: 'It is not all pleasure, this exploration.'

On 20 April, 'I am excessively weak.' On the 21st he fainted and fell off his donkey. Susi and Chuma carried him to a hut and next day built a litter and conveyed him across a flooded plain to the next village. He was suffering acute dysenteric pains. At the end of two or three hours' march, all that he could put up with, his men built a shelter for the night. On the 26th, Susi was told to count the bags of beads remaining. He reported twelve. The Doctor instructed him to buy two tusks if the opportunity offered, which they could exchange at Ujiji for cloth to take them on to Zanzibar. The last words he wrote were on the 27th: 'Knocked up quite, and remain – recover – sent to buy milch goats. We are on the banks of the Molilamo.'

On the 29th he was carried, in great pain, across the Lulimala river, near Lake Benguela, while some of his men went ahead to build a hut for him in the village of the chief, Chitambo, in the district of Ilala. Here he was laid gently on a bed of sticks and grass, by now in a coma. In the afternoon he revived sufficiently to wind up his chronometer while Susi held it. Later he asked faintly: 'Is this the Luapula?' When Susi replied that it was not, 'How many days to the Luapula?' 'I think three days', Susi answered. A boy was sleeping inside the doorway of his hut, and an hour or so before dawn on 1 May 1873, summoned Susi and Chuma. Their leader was kneeling by the bedside with his grey head buried in his hands. He had come to the end of his last earthly journey.

Two days before his death Livingstone was ferried across the Lulimala river, near Lake Benguela, by this man who, ten years later, posed for his photograph.

The rest of the story is a saga in itself, but must be quickly told. The caravan was over a thousand marching miles from the coast, in unknown country seething with inter-tribal wars and despoiled by raiders. It was without a leader, without food and without guides. Somehow the men had to get back to Zanzibar, and not only that; they had, as they immediately decided, to take the white man's body with them as proof that they had not murdered or abandoned him.

Susi and Chuma assumed the leadership, helped by Jacob Wainwright, one of the men sent by Stanley, who could read and write. He made an inventory of the goods, and a mourning ceremony was observed by the people of Chitambo's village. The heart and viscera were cut out of the body and buried in a tin box under a large *mvula* tree. The body itself was roughly but effectively embalmed, wrapped in the bark of a tree, lashed to a pole and hoisted on to the shoulders of bearers for the long march home.

Nine months later, the caravan reached the coast. The body, accompanied by Jacob Wainwright, duly arrived at Southampton and, on 18 April 1874, was buried amid national mourning in Westminster Abbey. Livingstone's old friends Steele, Oswell, Webb, Young, Waller and Kirk acted as pall-bearers, together with Henry Stanley and Jacob Wainwright. Susi and Chuma, the former wood-cutter and the freed slave from the Shiré, were brought to England a few months later to tell their story and to receive their reward.

If Livingstone had not got himself hopelessly entangled in the swamps, 'sponges' and rivers of Lake Banguelu, would he have 'completed the work' and found those 'ancient fountains', elusive as the Holy Grail? He would have seen the Luapula, twice as broad as the Zambesi where it issues from the south-west corner of Lake Banguelu, followed it down to Lake Mweru and for a second time seen it issue as the Lualaba to flow away to the north. Springs he might have found in Katanga, but not the four placed like some astrological symbol with a mound between. Sooner or later he must have realised, as perhaps he always knew in his heart of hearts, that he was tracing the sources not of the Nile but of the Congo. So, either way, his life must have ended in disappointment and failure. He had failed to find the sources of the Nile; he had failed to put an end to the slave trade; he had failed to establish the permanent missions he had so yearned to see. He had failed as

OPPOSITE The Doctor's heart and viscera were buried in a tin box underneath a tree in Chitambo's village in the district of Ilala. The portion of the tree bearing this inscription is now preserved in London by the Royal Geographical Society.

The End of the Road

Livingstone's funeral at Westminster Abbey was a day
of national mourning. It was not only for his
geographical discoveries that he was revered and would
be remembered, but for his greatness of character.
On his tombstone are the words he had addressed to the
New York Herald: 'May Heaven's rich blessing come
down on everyone – American, English, Turk – who
will help heal this Open Sore of the World'.

BELOW Among the pall-bearers was his old friend
William Webb at whose home, Newstead Abbey, he
had written his account of the Zambesi Expedition.
This photograph includes Mr and Mrs Webb, Susi and
Chuma, and his friend and fellow-missionary Horace
Waller. Waller subsequently edited the *Last Journal*

OPPOSITE ABOVE Invitation to Livingstone's
funeral at Westminster Abbey.

OPPOSITE BELOW Livingstone's coffin
in the Map Room of the Royal Geographical
Society, Savile Row.

FUNERAL OF DR LIVINGSTONE.

WESTMINSTER ABBEY,

Saturday, April 18th, 1874,

at 1-0 precisely.

𝕬𝖉𝖒𝖎𝖙 𝖙𝖍𝖊 𝕭𝖊𝖆𝖗𝖊𝖗 AT 12-30, TO THE **CHOIR.**

Entrance by the West Cloister Door, Dean's Yard.

A. P. STANLEY, (*Dean.*)

N.B.—No Person will be admitted except in Mourning.

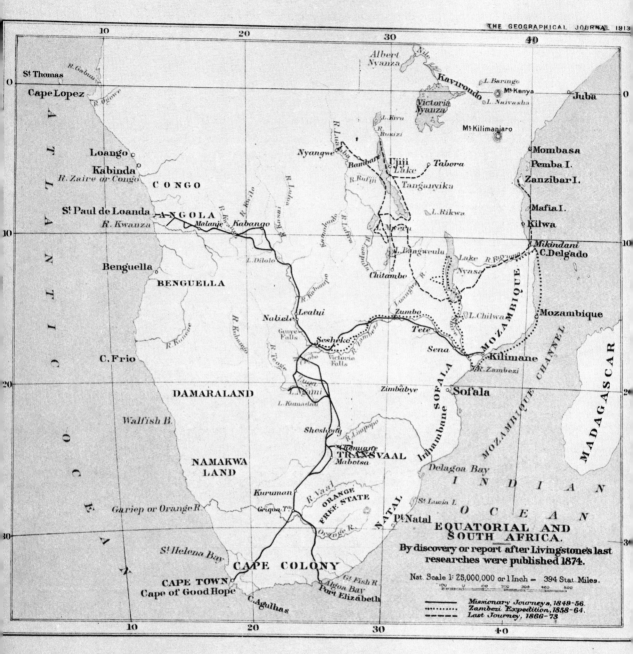

EQUATORIAL AND
SOUTH AFRICA

By discovery or report after Livingstone's last
researches were published 1874.

Nat. Scale 1: 25,000,000 or 1 Inch = 394 Stat. Miles.

——————— Missionary Journeys, 1849-56.
·················· Zambezi Expedition, 1858-64.
– – – – – – – Last Journey, 1866-73.

EQUATORIAL AND
SOUTH AFRICA
Johnston.

graphical Society

an evangelist. He had failed as a husband and a father. The one field he had not failed in was as a Christian, but his humility would not allow him to be, in his own estimation, more than 'a guilty, weak and helpless worm'.

'The evil that men do lives after them; the good is oft interred with their bones.' With David Livingstone, it was the other way round. The evil, if there was any, was buried with him; the good lived on, grew and triumphed. From the *mvula* tree in Ilala an influence radiated throughout Africa and the civilised world that in the end achieved all the ends to which he had dedicated his life. Within two months of his burial, the Sultan of Zanzibar yielded to pressure applied by John Kirk and signed a treaty prohibiting the export of slaves from his domains. The great slave market in his capital was closed, and before many years the Arab slave-trade ended. It was the influence of Livingstone – the impact of his writings, the force of his character and the tragedy of his death – that worked so powerfully on British public opinion as to oblige its government to take action which would heal 'the Open Sore of the World'.

His other aims were also, in the main, achieved. The mission that had failed so tragically on the Shiré was re-established on the shores of Lake Nyasa, and influenced strongly the development of the country known first as Nyasaland, then as Malawi. Within a century of his death, churches, cathedrals and African clergy and their flocks were scattered over the great areas of forest, swamp and desert into which he had been the first Christian to go. As a geographer he is said to have traversed, on foot and on the backs of oxen or donkeys, at least thirty thousand miles, and to have added to the known and measured parts of the planet about a million square miles. With his accurate and sympathetic observations on natural history, he enriched man's store of knowledge of his own environment. Tenacity of purpose, courage in adversity, humility of spirit and an abiding love for his fellow-men that the extremes of cruelty, greed and beastliness he saw in action never turned to cynicism or despair: these are the qualities for which he will be remembered, even when new sores open, as they have and will, in a continent which he loved, in sickness and in health, from the depths of his heart.

OPPOSITE During twenty-five years of exploration, all on foot or the backs of oxen or donkeys, Livingstone did more than any other man, before or since, to map the interior of Africa. This shows his main journeys, and may be contrasted with the map on page 27 of southern Africa at the time of his arrival.

Select Bibliography

Blaikie, W.G., *Personal Life of David Livingstone*. John Murray Ltd., 1880.

Campbell, R.J., *Livingstone*. Ernest Benn Ltd., 1929.

Coupland, R., *Kirk on the Zambesi*. Oxford University Press, 1928.
Livingstone's Last Journey. William Collins Son & Co., 1945.

Debenham, F., *The Way to Ilala*. Longman Group Ltd., 1955.

Gelfand, M., *Livingstone the Doctor*. Blackwell Scientific Publications Ltd., 1957.

Johnston, H.H., *Livingstone and The Exploration of Central Africa*. George Philip & Son Ltd., 1891.

Livingstone, D., *Missionary Travels and Researches in South Africa*. John Murray Ltd., 1857.
Narrative of an Expedition to the Zambesi and its Tributaries. John Murray Ltd., 1865.
Last Journals, ed. H.Waller. John Murray Ltd., 1874.
Family Letters, 1841-56. Chatto & Windus Ltd., 1959.
Cambridge Lectures, ed. W.Monk. Deighton Bell, 1860.

Oswell, W.E., *William Cotton Oswell*. William Heinemann Ltd., 1900.

Schapera, I., *Apprentice at Kuruman*. Oppenheimer Series, 1951.
(ed.) *Livingstone's Private Journals, 1851-53*. Chatto & Windus Ltd., 1960.
(ed.) *Livingstone's African Journal, 1853-56*. Chatto & Windus Ltd., 1963.

Seaver, George., *David Livingstone: His Life and Letters*. Lutterworth, 1957.

Smith, E.W., *Robert Moffat*. S.C.M. Press Ltd., 1925.

Stanley, H.M., *How I Found Livingstone*. Sampson Low, 1872.
Autobiography. Sampson Low, 1909.

Wallis, J.P.R. (ed.) *The Zambesi Expedition of David Livingstone, 1858-63*. Central African Archives No. 9. Chatto & Windus, 1956.

List of Illustrations

2 Portrait of Livingstone by Monson, 1851, *Royal Geographical Society.*
3 'Unlocking Central Africa', *Mary Evans Picture Library*
10–11 View of Kuruman, *Congregational Council for World Mission*
14 Mr Moffat, *Radio Times Hulton Picture Library*
14 Mrs Moffat, *Radio Times Hulton Picture Library*
15 Moffat's mission at Kuruman, *United Society for the Propagation of the Gospel*
16 Room where Livingstone was born, *Mary Evans Picture Library*
17 Livingstone's birthplace at Blantyre, *Mansell Collection*
18 Livingstone's schoolteacher, Mr Skimming, with his wife, *Scottish National Memorial to David Livingstone Trust*
19 Livingstone's birthplace and the factory where he worked as a young boy, *Mary Evans Picture Library*
20 Anderson College, Glasgow, *Scottish National Memorial to David Livingstone Trust*
23 Port Elizabeth, South Africa by T.Baines, *Courtauld Institute of Art*
24 Mission at Kuruman Station, *Congregational Council for World Mission*
25 Miniature of Livingstone painted before he sailed to Africa, *Congregational Council for World Mission*
26 A Cape wagon, *Scottish National Memorial to David Livingstone Trust*
27 Map of South Africa, 1840, *Royal Geographical Society*
30–1 Livingstone grappling with a lion, *Mary Evans Picture Library*
33 Mary Moffat Livingstone, *Scottish National Memorial to David Livingstone Trust*
34 Boer hunters, *Radio Times Hulton Picture Library*
35 Chief Sechele and his wife, *Congregational Council for World Mission*
36–7 South-west angle of Lake Ngami by T.Baines, *Die Africana Museum, Johannesburg*
38 William Cotton Oswell, frontispiece to his biography by his eldest son W.E.Oswell
41 The arrival at Lake Ngami of Livingstone, Oswell and party in 1850, *Radio Times Hulton Picture Library*
41 Lake Ngami, discovered by Oswell, Murray and Livingstone, *Mary Evans Picture Library*
42 Lechwe and poku, *Radio Times Hulton Picture Library*
44 Bushmen's temporary camp, *Mary Evans Pciture Library*
45 Map of Livingstone's first expedition, 1849–56 *Design Practitioners*
46 David Livingstone by Henry Phillips, 1857, *Radio Times Hulton Picture Library*
50–1 Cape Town and the Table Mountain, *Mary Evans Picture Library*
52 Livingstone's vocabulary of Tswana dialect, *South African Library*
53 Sir Thomas Maclear, *Scottish National Memorial to David Livingstone Trust*
54 Makololo domestic scene, *Mary Evans Picture Library*
56 J.J.Freeman, *Congregational Council for World Mission*
58 Feasting on a hippopotamus, photographer A.C.COOPER LTD., *United Society for the Propagation of the Gospel*
60–1 Section of autograph map of the central African rivers, *Scottish National Memorial to David Livingstone Trust*
64 Photograph taken by Dr Kirk of tropical undergrowth, *Congregational Council for World Mission*
66–7 Victoria Falls with stampeding buffaloes, *Royal Geographic Society*
68 Shipping slaves in west Africa, *Church Missionary Society*

71 Norman B.Bedingfeld, *Radio Times Hulton Picture Library*

73 St Paul de Loanda, from a sketch by Capt. H. Need, *Radio Times Hulton Picture Library*

74–5 Livingstone's map of the central river systems, *National Library of Scotland*

78–9 Kebrabasa Rapids, *Royal Geographical Society*

82–3 Invitation to a meeting with Livingstone at Blantyre, *Scottish National Memorial to David Livingstone Trust*

85 Victoria Falls on the Zambesi, *Radio Times Hulton Picture Library*

87 Mode of salutation from Kingston and Low's *Great African Travellers . . . 1890*, photographer JOHN R. FREEMAN AND CO. LTD.

90–1 The Zambesi river, Tete, 1859, *Royal Geographical Society*

93 Sketch of Livingstone's journeys in central South Africa, by John Snow, 1857, *South African Library*

97 A native of Tete, *Royal Geographical Society*

99 Murcheson, *Radio Times Hulton Picture Library*; Rae, *Royal Geographical Society*; Thornton, *National Archives of Rhodesia*; Baines, Kirk and Tidman, *Livingstone Memorial, Blantyre*

100 Zambesi natives with Perry, *Royal Geographical Society*

102 David Livingstone, 1897, *National Portrait Gallery*

102 Freedom of the city granted to David Livingstone, *Scottish National Memorial to David Livingstone Trust*

103 David Livingstone with a neighbour during his stay in England, *Congregational Council for World Mission*

103 Livingstone surrounded by his wife and children, *Scottish National Memorial to David Livingstone Trust*

104 Shipping the *Ma-Robert* for use on the Expedition at Birkenhead, *Radio Times Hulton Picture Library*

106–7 Elephants in the shallows of the Shiré river, *Royal Geographical Society*

109 Poling up the Zambesi by T.Baines, *Scottish National Memorial to David Livingstone Trust*

109 Bark cloth tree by T.Baines, *Scottish National Memorial to David Livingstone Trust*

111 David Livingstone, *Royal Geographic Society*

112 The *Ma-Robert* aground, 1858, by T.Baines, *Royal Geographical Society*

114 St George's Street and the Cathedral, Capetown, *Mary Evans Picture Library*

115 Pandamus near the Kongone Canal, plate from David and Charles Livingstone's *Zambesi Expedition*, 1865

116 Livingstone's station at mouth of the Kongone river, *Mary Evans Picture Library*

118 Kebrabasa Rapids, *South African Library*

120 The *Ma-Robert* in the Zambesi, from David and Charles Livingstone's *Zambesi Expedition*, 1865

122 Murchisons Falls by Mellor

123 Manganja woman, from David and Charles Livingstone's *Zambesi Expedition*, 1865

123 The *Ma-Robert*, *Mary Evans Picture Library*

125 Working a coal seam near Tete by T.Baines, *Royal Geographical Society*

126 Photograph by Dr Kirk of the Portuguese house where he and Livingstone lived, *Congregational Council for World Mission*

127 Alphabetical dictionary of Tete tribes, *South African Library*

131 Map of Livingstone's second expedition, 1858-64

132 Carriers with elephant tusks, *Congregational Council for World Mission*

133 Black Arabs of Zanzibar from Stanley's book on Livingstone and his journeys and discoveries in Central Africa, 1884, *Radio Times Hulton Picture Library*

135 Victoria Falls by T.Baines, *Courtauld Institute of Art*

136–7 Victoria Falls photographed by W.F.Fry, 1892, *Royal Geographical Society*

138–9 Drawing of a slave gang, photographer A.C.COOPER LTD., *United Society for the Propagation of the Gospel*

141 Bishop Gray's residence, photographer A.C.COOPER LTD., *United Society for the Propagation of the Gospel*

143 Bishop Mackenzie, photographer A.C.COOPER LTD., *United Society for the Propagation of the Gospel*

144 Livingstone freeing slaves, *The Bettman Archive, Inc.*

146 Missionaries buying food from the natives of Chibisia, photographer A.C.COOPER LTD., *United Society for the Propagation of the Gospel*

148–9 *Lady Nyassa*, Livingstone's steamer, *Mary Evans Picture Library*

152 Mary Moffat Livingstone's grave at Shupanga, photographer A.C.COOPER LTD., *United Society for the Propagation of the Gospel*

153 *Lady Nyassa* under construction, *Congregational Council for World Mission*

157 Chuma, one of Livingstone's favourite attendants, *Mansell Collection*

158 Susi, plate from Stanley's book on Livingstone and his journeys and discoveries in Central Africa, 1884, *Radio Times Hulton Picture Library*

158 A slave gang in Zanzibar, *Mary Evans Picture Library*

159 A slave-ship, *Mary Evans Picture Library*

159 Native village raided by slavers, *Congregational Council for World Mission*

161 Livingstone's sketch of the Falls, *Royal Geographical Society*

161 Extracts from Livingstone's notebook of 1859, *Scottish National Memorial to David Livingstone Trust*

162–3 Extracts from Livingstone's notebooks, *Scottish National Memorial to David Livingstone Trust*

164 Malo Ruo, 1863, watercolour by Mellor, *United Society for the Propagation of the Gospel*

166 Livingstone at BA meeting in Bath, *Royal Geographical Society*

169 Livingstone with Anna Mary, his youngest daughter, *Royal Geographical Society*

170 Major Frank Varden with Livingstone, *Scottish National Memorial to David Livingstone Trust*

171 Robert Moffat Livingstone, *Congregational Council for World Mission*

173 First visit to Chibisa, *United Society for the Propagation of the Gospel*

173 Native dance, *United Society for the Propagation of the Gospel*

174 Fishing at Rovuma, plate from David and Charles Livingstone's *Zambesi Expedition*, 1865

175 Chumah and Susi, *Radio Times Hulton Picture Library*

176 Evening halt, *United Society for the Propagation of the Gospel*

176 Pa Ruo, Shiré, *United Society for the Propagation of the Gospel*

179 An Arab dhow, *Congregational Council for World Mission*

180 Mr Young at a meeting of the Royal Geographical Society, 1868, *Radio Times Hulton Picture Library*

181 Search for Livingstone, *Mary Evans Picture Library*

183 Extracts from Livingstone's notebooks, *Scottish National Memorial to David Livingstone Trust*

185 Map of Livingstone's third expedition, 1866-73

187 Village scene from Stanley's book on Livingstone and his journeys and discoveries in Central Africa, 1884, *Radio Times Hulton Picture Library*

188 Missionary preaching, *South African Library*

190–1 Jacob Wainwright and the body of Livingstone, *Radio Times Hulton Picture Library*

197 Henry Morton Stanley, *Mary Evans Picture Library*

198 Gordon Bennett, *Mary Evans Picture Library*

200 Livingstone and Stanley on the Rusiji, *Radio Times Hulton Picture Library*

201 Livingstone's house at Ujiji, *Mansell Collection*

203 Henry Morton Stanley, *Mansell Collection*

205 Livingstone's last journal, *The Scottish National Memorial to David Livingstone Trust*

206 Chuma and Susi, *Scottish National Memorial to David Livingstone Trust*

211 The native who ferried Livingstone across the Lulimala, *Royal Geographical Society*

213 Old Chitambo, *Radio Times Hulton Picture Library*

214 Newstead Abbey, *Congregational Council for World Mission*

215 Invitation to Livingstone's funeral, *Scottish National Memorial to David Livingstone*

215 Livingstone's Coffin, *Royal Geographical Society*

216 Map of equatorial and south Africa, *Royal Geographical Society*

Index

African Association, 12
Ajawa Tribe, 142, 145, 147
Amoda, 172, 178, 184, 210

Baines, Thomas, 98, 117, 123, 124, 129
Banguelu, Lake, 156, 186, 205, 207, 213
Barotseland, 57, 72, 80
Batonga, 86
Bechuana Tribes, 28, 34, 43, 105,
    Bakwena, 26, 29, 53
    Bagalaka, 32
    Bakalahari, 39, 40
Bedingfeld, Lieutenant Norman, 71, 76, 98, 114–17
Bennett, James Gordon Jnr., 199
Boers, 32, 43, 52
Bogharib, Mohamed, 188, 193
British Empire, 105
Bruce, James, 13
Burrup, Mr, 150, 151
Bushmen, 43

Cape Town, 24, 49
Cassenge, 69
Chambezi River, 182, 184, 205
Chibisa, 122, 124, 128, 141, 151, 154
Chiboque Tribe, 65
Chitamba, 184
Chitane, 172, 178, 181
Chobe River, 44, 47, 48, 84
Chuma, 142, 156, 172, 178, 184, 194 et seq.
Clarendon, Earl of, 98, 101, 108
Congo River, 64, 92, 175, 182, 206, 213
Cuango River, 68, 76

Cypriano, 69

Dilolo, Lake, 64, 77, 80

Edwards, Roger, 28, 29, 32

Gabriel, Edmund, 70, 77

Kafue River, 87
Kalahari Desert, 12, 24, 28, 38, 62
Kebrabasa Rapids, 89, 117, 118, 135
Kirk, John, 98, 108, 117, 119, 122, 126, 128, 129, 137, 145, 147, 151 et seq. 168, 213
Kolobeng, 32, 34, 39, 40, 43, 52
Kongone River, 113, 123, 155, 156
Kuruman Missionary Station, 24, 29, 32, 51, 52, 54, 113, 134

Lady Nyassa, 129, 150, 152, 154, 156, 157, 160, 168, 172
Lander, Richard, 12
Last Journals, 182
Limpopo River, 32
Linyanti, 48, 55, 57, 72, 81, 84, 130
Livingstone, Agnes, 32, 152, 167
Livingstone, Anna Mary, 113, 151, 165
Livingstone, Charles, 98, 117, 123, 124, 126, 130, 145, 153 et seq., 171
Livingstone, David, early life, 13; education, 20; entry into London Missionary Society, 21; character of, 22, 47; qualifies as doctor, 22; ordained a missionary, 23; embarks for South Africa, 23; arrives at Kuruman, 24; Moffat's influence on, 24; first African

trek, 26; among the Bechuana tribes, 26; friendship with Bakwena chief Sechele, 27; introduction to African travel, 28; sites missionary at Mabotsa, 28; encounters lion, 29; convalesces at Kuruman, 29; marries Mary Moffat, 32; opinions of the Boers, 32, 53; baptises his only convert, 34; friendship with Captain Steele, 35; relationship with Oswell, 39; meets Sebituane, 44; discovers Zambesi, 48; relationship with Thomas Maclear, 52; becomes doubtful, 54; contracts African fever,55; becomes dedicated to the abolition of slavery, 56; abhors native savagery, 57; determines to open path to the interior, 59; suffers chronic Malaria, 62; chronicles flora and fauna encountered, 62, 72; reaches rain forests of Central Africa, 63; plagued by illness, 65; Makololo pledge loyalty to, 68; suffers chronic dysentery, 70; sets out to course the Zambesi, 72; bravery, 77, 88; receives gold medal from R.G.S., 81; discovers Victoria Falls, 84; returns to England a hero, 91; writes a book, 92, 94; receives two fellowships, 92; reawakens European awareness of Central Africa, 92; reunited with family, 94; becomes a public idol, 95; London Missionary Society withdraws support, 96; visits Foreign Secretary, the Earl of Clarendon and resigns from London Missionary Society, 98; prepares for next expedition, 98; plans diplomatic strategy to handle Portugal, 101; delivers lecture at Cambridge, 105; is received by the Queen, 105; returns to Africa, 110; launches Ma-Robert, 114; difficulties with Bedingfeld, 114; investigates the Kebrabasa Rapids, 117; explores the Shiré River, 122 et seq.; dispute with Baines, 124; criticisms of, 124; attempts at abolishing slavery, 129;

commissions new boat, 129; realises Charles' failings, 130; rewards of discoveries, 140; explores Lake Nyasa, 145; sadness at death of wife, 151; attacked by tribesmen, 153; sails to Bombay, 156; receives his second heroic welcome home, 165; addresses the British Association, 165; writes his second book, 165; sells Lady Nyassa, 172; recruits his team for another expedition in Bombay and Zanzibar, 172; thought dead, 178; is robbed of his medicine chest, 181; ill again, 186; determines to trace the source of the Nile, 192; meets and establishes rapport with Stanley, 196; sets out on last journey, 206; lost, 208; death of, 211; the influence of, 217

Livingstone, Janet, 96
Livingstone, John, 207
Livingstone, Mary, 32, 34, 40, 42, 48, 49, 51, 94, 110, 150
Livingstone, Neil, 94
Livingstone, Robert Moffat, 32, 47, 171
Livingstone, Thomas Steele, 35
Livingstone, William Oswell, 49, 110
London Missionary Society, 21, 91, 94, 96, 98
Lualaba, 156, 192, 193, 195, 205, 213
Luanda, 70 et seq.
Luangwa River, 88
Luapula River, 184, 213

Mabotsa Missionary site, 28, 32
Mackenzie, Charles, Bishop, 140, 147, 151, 168
Maclear, Thomas, 52, 73, 77
Magomero, 145, 150, 154, 156
Makololo Tribe, 38, 48, 55, 62 passim
Mambari Tribe, 55
Manganja Tribe, 142
Ma-Robert, 101, 114, 117, 121, 122, 129, 140
Matipa, Chief, 208, 209
Mebalwe, 29
Missionary Researches and Travels in South Africa, 92

Moffat, John, 96
Moffat, Robert, 22, 24, 34, 51, 113
Moore, Joseph, 21
Murchison Rapids, 122, 155
Murchison, Sir Roderick, 80, 91,
    98, 165
Murray, Mungo, 39
Musa, 178, 180
Mweru, Lake, 156, 184, 213

*Narrative of an Expedition to the
    Zambesi and its tributaries*, 167
New York Herald, 199
Ngami, Lake, 39
Ngoni Tribe, 155
Niger River, 12
Nile River, 175, 182, 192, 205, 213
Nitata Bay, 147
Nunes, Colonel, 91
Nyasa, Lake, 128, 145, 174, 178,
    180

Oswell, William Cotton, 39, 43, 44,
    47, 49, 167, 213

Park, Mungo, 12
Pearl, 105, 113
Pioneer, 140, 145, 147, 150 *et seq.*
Pires, Colonel, 76
Pitsane, 80, 81
Port Elizabeth, 23
Punch, 128, 202

Quilemane, 91, 104

Rae, George, 98, 117, 123, 128,
    129, 155, 156
Rovuma, 140, 153, 174
Royal Geographical Society, 81, 91,
    168

Sebituane, Chief, 38, 44, 47
Secard, Major, 89, 117, 142
Sechele, Chief, 28, 32, 34, 40, 53

Sekelutu, Chief, 55, 57, 81, 84, 86,
    91, 134
Sekwetu, 91
Shiré, 122, 128, 140, 152, 154,
    178
Shobo, 43-4
'Sinbad,' 64, 65, 77, 80
Slave-trade, 55, 63, 69, 91, 101,
    104, 108, 128, 132, 141, 142, 147,
    165, 177, 178, 204, 217
Stanley, Henry Morton, 196 *et seq.*,
    213
Susi, 172, 178, 184, 194 *et seq.*

Tanganyika, Lake, 182, 188, 189,
    202, 207
Tete, 12, 86, 89, 101, 104, 118, 122,
    123, 137
Thornton, Richard, 98, 124, 154
Tidman, Arthur, 94

Ujiji, 182, 188, 196
Universities Mission to Central
    Africa, 105, 156
Unyanyembe, 203, 206

Victoria Falls, 84
Victoria, Queen, 105, 134

Wainwright, Jacob, 213
Webb, William, 167, 213
Westminster Abbey, 213
Wikitani, 172
Wilson, Captain, 151

Young, Edward, 178
Young, James, 20, 87, 121, 168,
    213

Zambesi River, 48, 56, 62, 64, 72,
    76, 77, 84, 88, 92, 113, 122, 140,
    154, 175
Zanzibar, 156, 157, 182, 213
Zouga River, 39, 40, 49

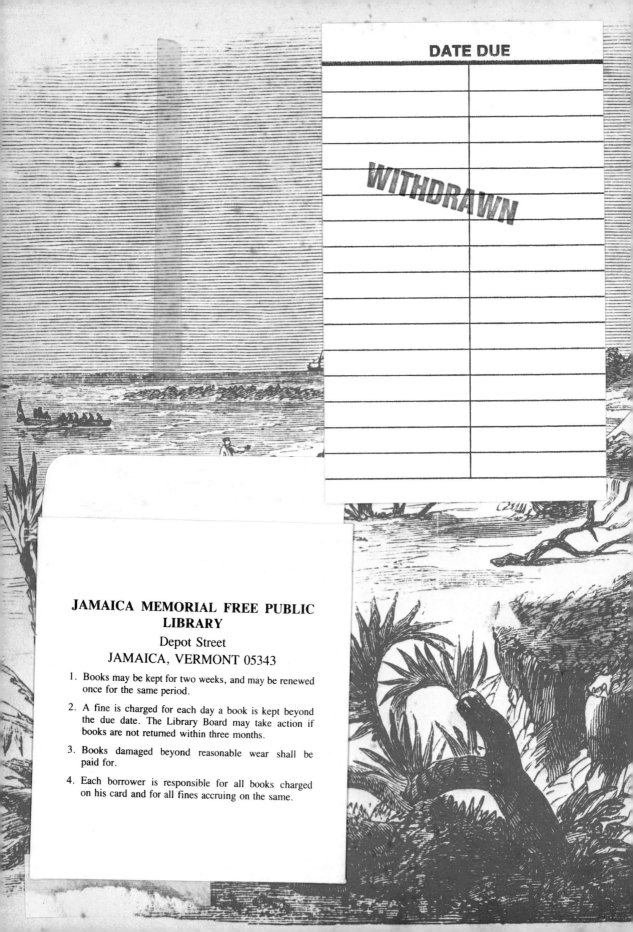

DATE DUE

WITHDRAWN